Relationship
Building Bridges to Connect People

Randy M. Clendenin, MA

Martha W. Homme, MA

© 2002, Randy Clendenin, 42 Goldenrod Drive, Whispering Pines, NC 28327

© 2002, Martha Homme, 480 Spring Lake Drive, Pinehurst, NC 28374

Copyright © 2002 by Randy M. Clendenin, MA.,
and Martha W. Homme, MA

Relationship
by Randy M. Clendenin, MA., and Martha W. Homme, MA

Printed in the United States of America

Library of Congress Control Number: 2002108867
ISBN 1-591601-48-7

All rights reserved. No part of this publication may be reproduced or transmitted in any form or by any means without written permission of the publisher.

Unless otherwise indicated, Bible quotations are taken from the New International Version. Copyright © 1973, 1978, 1984 by International Bible Society.

Xulon Press
11350 Random Hills Road
Suite 800
Fairfax, VA 22030
(703) 279-6511
XulonPress.com

To order additional copies, call 1-866-909-BOOK (2665).

Table of Contents

Acknowledgments vii

Foreword ix

Introduction xi

The Life in Christ Bridge 13

The Bridges:

    Authenticity 23

    Communication 35

    Compassion 45

    Contentment 55

    Forgiveness 67

    Grace 77

    Hope 87

    Hospitality 99

    Impartiality 109

Integrity 117

Intimacy 129

Love 139

Prayer 153

Transparency 167

Trust 179

Building Bridges: A Story 189

Notes 191

Scripture References 197

About BridgeBuilder Ministries International 239

Acknowledgments

We wish to express our thanks and gratitude to the following special people who helped make this book possible:

Douglas R. Stalls, MA EEd, our editor, reader and friend

Suzanne Clendenin, Randy's wife, soulmate and friend, who not only contributed *The Bridge of Hospitality,* but practices it continually

John Homme, Martha's husband, protector and friend, whose computer expertise transformed the messages of this book into a manuscript

Foreword

Relationship: Building Bridges to Connect People is a timely tool for the Kingdom of God. I believe Randy Clendenin and Martha Homme have listened to God and responded with this fine work.

Building Bridges is written with our American culture in mind. There is no question that the greatest approach of sharing our faith is through relationship building. The Apostle Paul writes: "We loved you so much that we were delighted to share with you not only the gospel of God but our lives as well" (1 Thessalonians 2:8 NIV).

Relationship building requires sharing our lives with others. To share our lives effectively with others requires connecting to God and people. That is what this book is all about. Not only does this material show how to build bridges through practical biblical strategies, it shows how to cross the bridges of life. It demonstrates how we can connect with others while growing in our relationship with Christ.

Dr. Jimmy Ray Lee
President
Turning Point Ministries, Inc.

Introduction

In *On the Anvil: Stories On Being Shaped Into God's Image,* Max Lucado tells the story of George, an acquaintance he made while living in Miami.[1] Although Max and George came from quite different worlds, "there was something profound about George that made me want to visit him." One summer day during a visit with George, Max realized what it was. That day George had something he wanted to show Max. That something was George's friend Ralph who had come to visit. Proudly introducing Ralph to Max, George said, "My most valued possession is my buddy, Ralph." "Two crusty old travelers on the back curve of life's circle. They had found life's most precious element—a *relationship*."

Max goes on to concur with what we, the staff of *BridgeBuilder Ministries, International,* want to share with you through this workbook and our conferences and workshops:

"Our Master knew the value of a relationship. It was through relationships that he changed the world. His movement thrived not on personality or power but on championing the value of a person. He built *bridges* and crossed them. Touching the leper...uniting the estranged...exalting the prostitute. And what was that he said about loving your neighbor as yourself?"

The primary purpose of *BridgeBuilder Ministries International* is to build relational bridges, connecting people to impact the world for Christ. When Jesus was asked, "What is the greatest commandment?" He replied, "Love the Lord your God with all your heart, with all your soul, and with all your mind. This is the first and greatest commandment. And the second is like it; Love your neighbor as yourself" (Matthew 22:37). BMI's goal is to help fulfill these commands by equipping people to build interpersonal relationships based on biblical principles.

RELATIONSHIP: Building Bridges to Connect People is our beginning. This collection of studies on the foundational bridge, "Life in Christ" accompanied by fifteen relational bridges, is designed to be used in any of the following ways:

- As our conference workbook (for those of you who will be attending one of our conferences)
- As a small-group study guide in churches (e.g. Sunday classes or week -day small groups)
- As an individual Bible study guide

For each *bridge*, we share a key scripture, an overview followed by "Core Concepts". We then launch you or your small group into a study of scriptures related to each bridge ("Scriptural Insights") and personalization of the scriptures and core concepts through "Focused Application".

It is our prayer that your journey through *RELATIONSHIP: Building Bridges to Connect People* will draw you closer to *the* Bridgebuilder, *Jesus* Christ, and will enhance your relationship with others.

CHAPTER 1

The Life in Christ Bridge

Key Scripture: "For every house is built by someone, but He who built all things is God." Heb 3:4

Overview:
Most of us are aware of a longing to be intimately connected with someone. Feelings of isolation create much pain. People look to others to fulfill them relationally and discover instead a deeper sense of emptiness. How do we find a connection? How do we experience relationship with others the way relationship was originally designed? The good news is God, the Master Builder, designed us for relationship. Since we are created in His image (Genesis 2:28), the beginning of connection, the beginning of relationship is to first connect to and relate to God. Christ is the connecting point between God and man. Through the cross Christ became the Bridge Builder. When we place our trust in Jesus Christ to be our Savior and Lord, we connect with God. Connecting with God gives us the ability, through Christ, to intimately connect with others.

The "Life in Christ" Bridge study guide explains:
- What happens at salvation: "Life in Christ"
- How "Life in Christ" makes intimate, meaningful relationships possible
- Why abiding in Christ is key to intimacy with God and our fellow man
- How to avoid involving yourself in empty relationships.

Scriptural references throughout provide biblical support for the bridge.

The "Focused Application" segment allows you to apply the biblical principles addressed in "Core Concepts" and "Scriptural Insights".

Core Concepts:

"The new birth is not just being reformed; it's being transformed. People are always making resolutions to do better, to change, and breaking those resolutions soon afterwards. But the Bible teaches us that through the new birth we can enter a new world." Billy Graham[1]

In the Old Testament, the Christian life is described as walking with God and obeying God's commands. In the New Testament, the Apostle Paul writes about an experience that revolutionizes our lives. "Therefore, if anyone is *in Christ*, he is a new creation; old things have passed away; behold, all things have become new" (II Corinthians 5:17). These two words "*in Christ*" comprise a brief, but most profound statement of the inexhaustible significance of the believer's *redemption*, which includes the following:

1. the believer's *security* in Christ, who bore in His body God's judgement against sin;
2. the believer's *acceptance* in Him with whom God alone is well pleased;
3. the believer's *future assurance* in Him who is the resurrection to eternal life, and
4. the believer's *participation* in the divine nature of Christ.

This new creation in II Corinthians 5:17 describes something that is created at a new level of excellence. It refers to *regeneration* or the *new birth*. (John 3:3) After a person is regenerated, old value systems, priorities, beliefs, loves and plans are transformed. Evil and sin are still present, but the believer sees them in a new perspective and they need no longer control him. The believer's new and constant perception of everything, including relationships with others, is a spiritual perception.

Life in Christ Makes Intimate, Meaningful Relationships Possible:

Robert McGee, in his best selling book, the *Search For Significance* discusses a very important concept regarding hindrances to building relationships. He brings into focus the amount of fear we are preoccupied with since "the fall" (Genesis 3). McGee writes about the fear of failure, fear of rejection, fear of punishment, and the fear of being known. He elaborates on the idea that the world insists people get their self worth from their performance plus others' opinions about them. We can see how this thinking could hamper greatly our ability to relate deeply with anyone, including God. McGee masterfully and scripturally refutes this idea. Instead, through the finished work of Jesus Christ on the cross, a person's self-worth can be totally based upon the unconditional love of God, the complete forgiveness of sins and the total acceptance that comes through believing in Jesus Christ as our Lord and Savior. At the point of salvation, through Christ, the believer can experience victory over his fears. This creates a very real possibility for a deeply loving relationship with God and others. [2]

The Bible says "There is no fear in love; but perfect love casts out fear, because fear involves torment. But he who fears has not been made perfect in love. We love Him because He first loved us." (I John 4:18-19) If we know and believe we are eternally loved by God through Christ and God's love will never let us go, we are far more poised to love others. Once love replaces our fears, connecting with others can become a reality.

Abiding in Christ is Key to Intimacy with God and Our Fellow Man:

God removes all things in the believer's life that would hinder meaningful relationships. He disciplines to cut away sin and hindrances that would drain spiritual life, just as the farmer removes anything on the branches that keeps them from bearing maximum fruit. The word *abide* (John 15) means to remain or stay around. The *remaining* is evidence that salvation has already taken place. The fruit or evidence of salvation is continuance in service to Him and His teaching. True believers obey the Lord's commands, submitting to His Word. Because of their commitment to God's Word, they are devoted to His will. The true believer lives according to the greatest commandment as specified by Jesus in Matthew 22:37: he is to love the Lord his God with all of his heart, soul and mind and his neighbor as himself. This is not emotional or mystical, but as defined in John 15, is obedience to Christ. When we are abiding in Christ we will relate to others in love; relationship will become the central focus in our lives. We will desire what God desires. The divine nature of Christ that resides in us will empower us to relate in love with others.

Avoid Involving Yourself in Empty Relationships:

Many of us settle for an empty religion based upon rules and outward perceptions. We have made an intellectual assent, settling for false substitute relationships. This lifestyle is difficult to avoid because it is the cultural norm. The majority of us fall victim to superficial relating. Larry Crabb describes in *Connecting* that we are disconnected souls.[3] Empty religion is not relational; it's more about portraying an image.

Be diligent, do not succumb to the inward and outward pressures of empty relationships, but rather believe that "Life in Christ" will place a desire in your heart for intimate oneness with God and with others within the body of Christ. Study the life of Christ and see how he related to his disciples and others. Be determined to see the value of others, listen carefully to people's words and seek to understand those around you. In doing these things, you are fulfilling the law of Christ that is love.

Scriptural Insights:

The focus of these scriptural references is to give you a biblical understanding of the "The Life in Christ Bridge". (Scriptures are printed in the back of the book.)

1. *Jn 1:12; Eph 1:4-7; Eph 2:8-10; 1 Peter 1:18,19*
Salvation is wholly of God by Grace on the basis of the redemption of Jesus Christ, the merit of His shed blood, and not on the basis of human merit or works.
According to these verses, what is your understanding of salvation through Jesus Christ?

2. *Jn 3:3-8; Titus 3:5*
Regeneration is a supernatural work of the Holy Spirit by which the divine nature and divine life are given.
Why is regeneration so important, when it comes to changing our attitude and behavior about relationship building?

3. *Luke 13:3; Acts 2:38, 3:19, 11:18*
Justification is an act of God (Romans 8:30,33) by which He declares righteous those who, through faith in Christ, repent of their sins and confess Him as sovereign Lord.
How would the above truth help us connect with Christ and others if we applied it to our lives?

4. *Acts 20:32; 1 Cor 1:2, 30, 6:11; Hebrews 2:11, 3:1*
Sanctification means every believer is set apart unto God by justification and is therefore declared to be holy. This sanctification is positional and instantaneous. The sanctification has to do with the believer's standing, not his present walk or condition.
According to these scriptures, when we find our life in Christ, are

we able to begin connecting with others as God originally designed?

Focused Application:
Put more practically, how do we allow Jesus Christ to build this "foundation bridge" so that connecting with others is possible.

I. How do we allow Jesus Christ to build the "foundational bridge", so that connection with others is possible?
A. Confess (*1 Jn 1:9*) our sins of trying to build a bridge apart from Christ and the supernatural power of His Spirit.

B. Repent (*Acts 3:19; Rev 2:5*) and recognize these attempts as sinning against God and others.

C. Renew our thinking (*2 Cor 10:5; Rom 12; Phil 4:8*) See the absolute need of having the mind of Christ. Also recognize the spiritual battle for the mind. Remember it all begins with our thinking.

D. Persevere (*Jas 1:2-4,*) pressing on and remaining utterly dependent upon Christ during times of trials and testing.

E. Rely upon the indwelling Holy Spirit (*Eph 4*). This is where the power lies to overcome temptation and to ultimately succeed in connecting.

F. Abide in Christ (*Jn 15*) allows the life in Christ to be our "foundational bridge". Coming to the realization that Christ is "The Bridge Builder" and only through Him can we experience connecting relationships with others.

Confess	Repent	Renew	Persevere	Rely on	Abide
		thinking		Holy Spirit	in Christ

Questions:
1. Using an X, indicate your current position on the Life in Christ Bridge.

2. What goal could you set to take the next step toward "connecting" in Christ?

II. Examples of our feeble attempts for relationship that lead only to emptiness (disconnectedness) include:
- We attempt to control/demand someone to love us.
- We believe a loving relationship is based upon what we can get from it.
- Our expectations are to have all of our known longings met.
- We self-protect, cover our flaws hoping not to be rejected.
- We promise security for the other person.
- We attempt to make the person feel absolutely significant.
- We demand the other person to make us feel secure.
- We demand the other person make us feel significant.
- We suggest that we can make the other person happy.
- We believe the other person can make us happy.
- We place too high a priority upon the physical appearance.
- We attempt through financial extravagance to buy our way into intimacy.
- We believe other things, outside of Christ, are common passions that will hold us together.

Place an X by the feeble attempts for relationship that you engage in.

What other feeble attempts at relationship do you need to add to this list?

III. Life in Christ involves allowing Jesus Christ, the "Bridge Builder", to connect us not only to God but also to one another.

Through the Cross, Jesus brings restoration:

The Life in Christ Bridge

A. Significance/value
B. Security
C. Forgiveness

D. Unconditional love
E. Grace
F. Mercy

G. Contentment
H. Compassion
I. Desire for Spiritual/Emotional Intimacy
J. The ability to be transparent
K. Truth
L. Trust

1. Which of the above are you experiencing currently?

2. Which of these would you like to experience today?

CHAPTER 2

The Bridge of Authenticity

Key Scripture: To do what is right and just is more acceptable to the Lord than sacrifice. Proverbs 21:3

Overview:
God created us to be in *relationship* with Him. *Authenticity* in our relationship with Him creates a sweet-smelling aroma and strengthens the potential for authentic relationship with others.

The "Bridge of Authenticity" study guide addresses the following:

- What it means to *be authentic*
- Relating authentically to God and Others
- The "How To's" and the "How Not To's" of Authenticity

Scriptural references throughout provide biblical support for the bridge.

The "Focused Application" segment allows you to apply the scriptural principles addressed in "Core Concepts" and "Scriptural Insights".

Core concepts:

"God designed us to yearn for open, honest, authentic relationships—'communal' relationships. But because we choose peacekeeping over truth-telling, we end up in 'pseudocommunal' relationships instead."[1] M. Scott Peck

What it means to be authentic:

Bill Hybels subtitled his small group interactions guide *Authenticity,* "Being Honest with God and Others."[2] The dictionary defines *authentic* as "something that conforms to what it is represented or claimed to be." That which is authentic is not false; it is genuine, trustworthy, entitled to acceptance or belief because of agreement with known facts or experience. The thesaurus lists accurate, bona fide, creditable, dependable, for real, legitimate, and reliable among the synonyms for authentic.

The prophet Jeremiah challenges us to authentic living. "If you have raced with men on foot, and they have wearied you, how will you compete with horses? And if in a safe land you fall down, how will you do in the jungle of the Jordan?" (Jeremiah 12:5). In *Run With the Horses*, Eugene Peterson's reflections on the life of Jeremiah, Peterson states, "the only way that any one of us can live at our best is in a life of radical faith in God. Every one of us needs to be stretched to live at our best, awakened out of dull moral habits, shaken out of petty and trivial busy-work."[3]

Dr. Richard Swenson, a Christian physician and futurist, best know for his book entitled *Margin,* in 1999 wrote *Hurtling Toward Oblivion,* a book about the economic, mathematical, social and other indicators that suggest we are truly living in the end times. After detailing these indicators, Swenson goes on to say "This book is not at all about fatalism or desperation. It is a call to authenticity." He defines authenticity as the congruence between what we believe and how we live. He then examines four aspects of the fully authentic life that will help us live ready: vision, values, relationships and lifestyle.[4]

In *The Safest Place on Earth,* a commentary on spiritual community, Larry Crabb contrasts flesh dynamics (the passion for self, the passion to control, the passion to define, and the passion of pressure) with spirit dynamics (the passion to worship, trust, grow and obey).[5] Flesh dynamics lead to inauthentic living; spirit dynamics, to authentic living.

Relating authentically to God:

In his best-selling book, *The Prayer of Jabez*, Bruce Wilkinson reminds us of the authentic relationship with God of a little-known Bible hero Jabez, a descendent of Judah. Jabez "was more honorable than his brothers" (I Chronicles 4:9) Jabez's acknowledgement of God as his true center led him to pray boldly for God to bless him, enlarge his territory (i.e. his bridges to others), to be with him in all he did, and to keep him from evil and harm. Why could Jabez pray so boldly? He had passed four tests of authentic living: the tests of devotion to God, being faithful in small things, being accessible to God in his heart and mind, and being a man of integrity.[6]

The Recabites (Jeremiah 35), a guild of wandering metal workers, was forced to come into the walls of Jerusalem during the Babylonian invasion of Judah for safety. While there, they were invited to lunch by Jeremiah and were offered wine to drink. Their cordial decline was insightful to Jeremiah. The Recabites were everyday evidence that ordinary people can live authentic lives, obedient to God's commands for them, rather than succumb to crowd pressures. Neither the hospitality of their kind host or the customs of the city distracted them from authentic living.

Relating authentically with God requires relationship. God asks us to be devoted to Him, faithful, obedient, and accessible; in return, He will "do immeasurably more than all we ask or imagine, according to his power that is at work within us" (Ephesians 3:20).

Relating authentically to others:

Paul's ministry in Thessalonica (1 Thessalonians 2: 1-12) illustrates three characteristics of authentically relating to others. Paul honestly reached out to the Thessalonians to share the gospel with them, in spite of the strong opposition and imprisonment he had experienced in Philippi (2:2). He willingly and gently entered into relationship with them: "We loved you so much that we were delighted to share with you not only the gospel of God but our lives as well, because you had become so dear to us (2:8). Third, he related to them with integrity: "You are witnesses, and so is God, of how holy, righteous and blameless we were among you who believed. For you know that we dealt with each of you as a father deals with his own children, encouraging, comforting and urging you to live lives worthy of God" (2:10-12).

This recent review of two Billy Graham "interviews", reminds us of our perhaps most authentic modern-day Christian:

"May We Nestle, Not Wrestle"

Last year I watched Billy Graham being interviewed by Oprah Winfrey on television. Oprah told him that in her childhood home, she use to watch him preach on a little black and white TV while sitting on a linoleum floor. She went on to tell viewers that in his lifetime Billy has preached to twenty million people around the world, not to mention the countless numbers who have heard him whenever his crusades are broadcast. When she asked if he got nervous before facing a crowd, Billy replied humbly, "No, I don't get nervous before crowds, but I did today before I was going to meet with you."

Oprah's show is broadcast to twenty million people every day. She is comfortable with famous stars and celebrities but seemed in awe of Dr. Billy Graham. When the interview ended, she told the audience, "You don't often see this on my show, but we're going to pray." Then she asked Billy to close in prayer. The camera panned the studio audience as they bowed their heads and closed their eyes just like in one of his crusades.

Oprah sang the first line from the song that is his hallmark "Just as I am, without a plea," misreading the line and singing off-key, but her voice was full of emotion and almost cracked. When Billy stood up after the show, instead of hugging her guest, Oprah's usual custom, she went over and just nestled against him. Billy wrapped his arm around her and pulled her under his shoulder. She stood in his fatherly embrace with a look of sheer contentment.

I once read the book "Nestle, Don't Wrestle" by Corrie Ten Boom. The power of nestling was evident on the TV screen that day. Billy Graham was not the least bit condemning, distant, or hesitant to embrace a public personality who may not fit the evangelistic mold. His grace and courage are sometimes stunning.

In an interview with Hugh Downs, on the 20/20 program, the subject turned to homosexuality. Hugh looked directly at Billy and said, "If you had a homosexual child, would you love him?" Billy didn't miss a beat. He replied with sincerity and gentleness, "Why, I would love that one even more."

The title of Billy's autobiography, "Just As I am,' says it all. His life goes before him speaking as eloquently as that charming southern drawl for which he is known. If, when I am eighty years old, my autobiography were to be titled "Just As I Am," I wonder how I would live now? Do I have the courage to be me? I'll never be a Billy Graham, the elegant man who draws people to the Lord through a simple one-point message, but I hope to be a person who is real and compassionate and who might draw people to nestle within God's embrace.

Billy complimented Oprah when asked what he was most thankful for; he said, "Salvation given to us in Jesus Christ" then added, and the way you have made people all over this country aware of the power of being grateful." When asked his secret of love, being married fifty-four years to the same person, he said, "Ruth and I are happily incompatible." How unexpected. We would all live more comfortably with everybody around us if we would find the strength in being grateful and happily incompatible. Let's take the things that set us apart, that make us different, (that make us authentic), that cause us to disagree, and make them an occasion to compliment each other and be thankful for each other. Let us be big enough to be smaller than our neighbor, spouse, friends, and strangers.

Every day, may we Nestle, not Wrestle!
>	Author Unknown

The "How To's" and the "How Not To's" of Authenticity:

Authenticity with God leads to authenticity with others. In *Authenticity: Being Honest With God and Others,* Bill Hybels shares the following three-phased discipline he uses to grow more authentic:
- Journaling and reflecting on yesterday,
- Praying using the simple four-step prayer (adoration, confession, thanksgiving and supplication),
- Seeking to quiet his heart and listen to God.[7]

Relating authentically to others is enhanced not only by our own authenticity, but also through knowing others' "lifestyles". "Lifestyle" refers to the ways one typically responds to what one has experienced. Paul Welter identified four elements or "living channels" of lifestyle: feeling, thinking, choosing and doing. Knowing the "living channel" strengths and weaknesses of those we desire authentic relationships with boosts the probability of relating authentically.[8]

Wearing masks and/or playing roles are the two deadliest hindrances to authentic relationships. Authentic persons fit the "what you see is what you get" profile. They do not hide behind or operate out of false facades or faulty missions. They are authentic because the messages they give, the behaviors they engage in are crystal clear, not cloudy; they are genuine and not contrived.

Scriptural Insights

The focus of these scriptural references is to give you a biblical understanding of the Bridge of Authenticity. (Scriptures are printed in the back of the book.)

1. *2 Co 10:7*
What is Paul's claim to authenticity in this verse?

2. *Da 2:1-11*
How does Daniel demonstrate authenticity in this passage?

3. *Mt 3:1-11 and Mt 11:1-15*
What does John the Baptist teach us about authenticity in these passages?

4. *Jn 3:21*
How does this verse define authentic living?

5. *Ac 9:26-27*
What characteristic of authenticity does Barnabas illustrate in these verses?

6. *Eph 4:23-26*
As "children of light", what attributes does Paul tell us we need to put off and what attributes are we to put on instead if we are to live authentically?

7. *Php 4:8*
Our actions follow our thoughts. What thoughts are we to fill our minds with if we are to live authentically?

8. *Mt 6:33*
How does this well known verse illustrate authenticity?

9. *Jer 17:9-10; 1 Sam 16:7*
What do these two scriptures about the heart tell us about God's criteria for authenticity?

Focused Application

I. List as many characteristics of an authentic relationship as you can.

What encourages you to authenticity?

What hinders your practice of authenticity?

II. In *Authenticity: Being Honest With God and Others* Bill Hybels shares the following three-phased discipline he uses to avoid inauthentic Christianity:
- Journaling and reflecting on yesterday
- Praying using the simple four-step prayer (adoration, confession, thanksgiving and supplication)
- Seeking to quiet his heart and listen to God

How might journaling enhance your potential for authenticity
- with God?

- with others?

What role(s) does prayer play in practicing authenticity?

Hybels indicates that " journaling and writing out my prayers slow

me down enough to hear God's still, small voice. The third step is to listen and ask God to speak to me." Hybels asks God the following questions:
- What is my next step in my relationship with you?
- What is the next step in the development of my character?
- What is the next step in my family life?
- What is the next step in my ministry?

What do you suppose would happen in your life if you were to regularly ask God these questions and listen for His response?

What additional questions would you want to ask?

III. The four "living channels" identified by Paul Welter in *How to Help a Friend* are listed below along with descriptions of people with strong channels and weak channels:

CHANNEL:	Person With Strong Channel:	Person With Weak Channel:
FEELING	Aware of own feelings; able to express them.	Does not know how to take own emotional pulse; may come across cold or inhibited
THINKING	Analytical; investigative frame of mind.	Unaware; impulsive
CHOOSING	Courageous; has a clear value structure.	Indecisive

DOING	Changes behavior when necessary.	Immobilized by deep feelings

What is your strongest "living channel"? Your weakest? How does being strong or weak in these "response-able" channels impact your ability to be authentic?

IV. Think back over the last week. Did you don any masks? If so, what were they and why did you feel the need to put them on? What impact did they have on your authenticity?

Which of the roles that you played during the past week were inauthentic? Why?

V. Re-read the story of Barnabas's encouragement of Paul in Acts 9: 26-27.

Who have been "Barnabases" in your life?

To whom might you be a Barnabas?

CHAPTER 3

The Bridge of Communication

Key Scripture: Do not let any unwholesome talk come out of your mouths, but only what is helpful for building others up, that it may impart grace to the hearers. Ephesians 4:29

Overview:

Communication is a master life skill. Relationships are destroyed on a regular basis between people due to absence of communication. Effective communication requires spiritual maturity and emotional healthiness. This bridge will define communication in a simplistic way: communication is "connecting" with another person. Connecting builds the bridge of understanding and encouragement. When communication is done ineffectively, it wounds, aggravates and drives people further apart. It can be discouraging if you are struggling in this area. Take courage. The Bridgebuilder, Jesus Christ, can help you and others build the bridge of communication.

The "Bridge of Communication" study guide addresses the following:
- Reasons communication is difficult
- How to become a stronger communicator
- Five components of effective communication

Scriptural references throughout provide Biblical support for the bridge.

The "Focused Application" segment allows you to apply the scriptural principles addressed in "Core Concepts" and "Scriptural Insights".

Core Concepts:
In order to become an effective communicator, we must first be absolutely convinced of the importance of connecting with one another. It is our tendency to speak too quickly, not speak at all or very little, listen to what we find interesting, or just not listen. We all wrestle with the idea of becoming effective communicators.

Reasons communication is difficult:

Our human nature battles with self-preoccupation. This condition can be traced back to "the fall". Adam and Eve chose to go against God's plan for them. Since this most significant event, humanity continues to struggle with being disconnected from each other. The most important element of "relationship" was interrupted. Adam and Eve lost their sense of communing with God and most likely with each other. The ability to remain vulnerable with God and each other was lost in a sea of fear, shame and guilt. Tension took the place of tranquility.

Until we come to Christ and receive a new life, we have no chance of getting past our own inabilities to communicate. Communication is difficult. It is a behavior we all long for; however, it goes against our fallen condition. To truly connect with someone requires getting past our fear, shame, and guilt. Difficult communication affects not only you, but everyone else as well. We all are bouncing off of each other until God changes our mindset about communication.

How to become a stronger communicator:

Becoming a stronger communicator starts with an understanding of the importance of effective communication. We must desire to practice this master life skill. Getting to this level of awareness requires seeing God's will for relationships. "Therefore, I urge you, brothers, in view of God's mercy, to offer your bodies as living sacrifices, holy and pleasing to God—this is your spiritual act of worship. Do not conform any longer to the pattern of this world, but be transformed by the renewing of your mind. Then you will be able to test and approve what God's will is—his good, pleasing and perfect will." (Romans 12:1-2)

Coming to a place of change and desiring to become connected, according to God's will, requires grateful obedience to what God has done for us through Jesus Christ. We must offer up ourselves for God's purposes. For those of us in Christ, the only acceptable worship is to offer ourselves completely to the Lord. We must be yielded to Him as an instrument of righteousness. We owe God our highest form of service. Christians should no longer conform to the world's values, such as every person for himself, but rather be transformed to a higher level of living. We should outwardly manifest our inner, redeemed natures in the context of relationship. This kind of transformation can only occur as the Holy Spirit changes our thinking through the study of scripture. The renewed mind is a mind saturated with and controlled by the Word of God. We must develop the mind of Christ and allow it to be represented in our communication.

In the following pages we will discuss some components of Christlike communication. It is amazing how rarely people really connect. Even within the body of Christ, we seem to overlook the tremendous importance of communicating with each other. It seems our attitude is, "We'll leave the responsibility of communicating with the experts." We choose consciously or unconsciously to live disconnected lives. When we do this, we are missing out on a central purpose for living. God created us to be in relationship with Him and each other. Until we come to this place of understanding and begin to walk in this wonderful truth, our lives will not be abundant.

Five components of effective communication:

Do you realize that every person you come in contact with has been emotionally wounded? Think about this. Every person, including those in your family, is struggling with various forms of fear. The fears of rejection, failure, punishment, and being found out are all real possibilities. People are fragile. We wear masks and often believe the lies: "I am self sufficient;" "I can handle anything;" "I don't need anybody;" "No one would love me if they really knew me." The most horrifying deception is, "I am not worthy of anyone wanting to connect with me."

The first component of effective communication is *realizing who we are in Christ*. The basis of our self-worth rests entirely upon Christ's finished work on the cross. We hold worth because God through Christ declares we are unconditionally loved, totally forgiven, and completely accepted. These liberating truths are the only truths that can bring us to a point of valuing others.

To connect with a person, we must first see our true value in Christ. Otherwise, we will fail to see other people's true value. When we recognize our true value in Christ, our motivation to communicate will be out of love rather than fear.

Communication begins when we bring each other out of hiding rather than promoting self-protection. We have to authentically care about others. Seeing people the way Jesus sees them is our first endeavor. This requires much humility and vulnerability when interacting with others.

Secondly, *engaged listening* is a way of valuing people. Most of us wrestle with the plague of thinking about what we are going to say while the other person is speaking. Many times we carelessly invalidate the other person's thoughts and feelings. Being an engaged listener is not a natural behavior. Our lives can be full of preoccupations and various forms of distractions. Listening requires self-discipline.

Connecting is more likely to occur when we practice engaged listening. Listening speaks volumes. It says to others, "I want to know you. I desire to discover who you are. I care about your innermost longings." Simply put, it makes people feel important when you listen to them. When people feel important, they desire to connect.

Clarification is our third important component of communication. Clarification is a behavior that ensures understanding between people. The art of asking questions is a learned skill. This will take time, discipline, energy, and much desire.

Knowing when to ask a question is key. Building trust with a person is a prerequisite. Not being too forceful is also important. Examples of clarification include asking: "What do you think about—?" "Tell me how you feel about—" Are you saying—?" "Let me see if I understand—"

Be patient with yourself. This process will take time. You will be motivated to continue maturing your clarification skills as you experience results from engaged listening.

Fourthly, *say what you mean and mean what you say.* In other words, plan your words carefully. The tongue can be an instrument of healing or a weapon of destruction. As stated earlier, all people have been wounded emotionally. Many times harsh words have caused these wounds. Communication is intended to connect you to others, not to drive them back into hiding. Gauge your words. Ask yourself the question, "Has this relationship progressed to a level that these words can be said or do they even need to be said?" Practice giving encouragement. Avoid words like "should", "ought", or "must". Our words are to be seasoned with grace. Be determined to speak words that bring life rather than death. If you have to speak hard words, and truth is often hard, make sure love is your motivation.

This leads to the fifth and final component in this study, *confrontation*. Confrontation usually has a negative connotation. Ron

Kraybill, a respected Christian mediator, has noted that effective confrontation is like a graceful dance from supportiveness to assertiveness and back again. The dance, which Kraybill refers to, may feel awkward at first for those who are just learning. However, perseverance pays off. With God's help you can learn to speak the truth in love by saying only what will build others up. Be quick to remind the person of his value and of your love for him. Avoid attacking the person; rather, attack the behavior. Care and compassion will be part of Christ-like confrontation. Let your anger be driven by your genuine concern for the person's highest good, rather than by a desire to "whip him into shape". It is God's job to change people, not ours.

Our motivation for confronting someone needs to be for the glory of God and for his or her highest good. This will create a healthy relationship between the other person and us. Confrontation involves honesty and a high desire for transparency. Always conclude the confrontation with reminding the person of his or her value. This will secure the connecting bridge between each of you.

Communication is a master life skill. It requires spiritual maturity, emotional wholeness, and an on-going desire to be like Christ. The benefits of developing Christ-like communication greatly exceed the effort and discipline required to do so. If in doubt, just ask a recipient of effective Christ-like interactions.

Scriptural Insights:

The focus of these scriptural references is to give you a biblical understanding of the "Bridge of Communication". (Scriptures are printed in the back of the book.)

1. *Jas 1:19*
What does God's Word instruct us to do in this verse?

2. *Pr 15:1; Eph 4:26*
How are we to handle anger?

3. *Ecc 12:10*
According to this particular verse, how important are our words?

4. *Pr 16:24; Pr 25:11*
How important are encouraging words?

5. *Isa 50:4*
How does this verse instruct us to counsel one another?

6. *Col 4:6*
What is our conversation to be *filled* with according to this verse?

7. *Jas 3*
Write out the main points James discusses in this chapter. How do they relate to effective communication?

Focused Application:

I. How effectively do you communicate with others?

0_____10

II. Which areas of communication do you struggle in and why?

III. Do you regularly practice listening skills? What makes listening difficult for you at times?

IV. Is valuing others easy for you? Why or why not? On what do you base your value?

V. Who do you know whom you consider a strong communicator? What are the characteristics of communication that you appreciate in them the most?

VI. How would a family member rate your communication skills?

0_____10

VII. What are some ways you could develop your communication skills?

VIII. Commit to finding an accountability person to assist you in becoming a better communicator. Meet with them on a regular basis.

IX. Consider your words. Do you encourage more than discourage others?

If you use discouraging words, what commitment will you make to speaking encouragement?

CHAPTER 4

The Bridge of Compassion

Key Scripture: All of you live in harmony with one another; be sympathetic; love as brothers, be compassionate and humble. Do not repay evil with evil or insult with insult, but with blessing, because to this you were called so that you may inherit a blessing.
—I Peter 3:8-9

Overview:
Compassion is a key player in the fleshing out of *relationship,* relationship with God and with each other. God's grace and mercy are prime examples of His compassion for us. We extend His relationship with us to others through the recognition of their brokenness and our willingness to 'be there' for them. The bridge of compassion is built on the footings and foundation of pain, suffering and our own life experiences.

"Compassion may seem safe. It may even have an appealing ring to it. But it has been known to start revolutions. And if you become addicted, nothing else satisfies. You will be different. You will be hooked for the rest of your life—like someone else I know... Christ."[1] Swindoll, the author of this statement, goes on to say, "It is doubtful that there is anything more basic, more Christlike, and therefore more Christian than compassion."

The Bridge of Compassion study guide addresses the following:
- What is compassion
- Prerequisites for showing compassion
- Parables and people of compassion in the scriptures
- How to demonstrate compassion

Scriptural references throughout provide biblical support for the bridge.

The "Focused Application" segment allows you to apply the scriptural principles addressed in "Core Concepts" and "Scriptural Insights".

Core Concepts:

"Lord, make me an instrument of Thy peace. Where there is hatred, let me sow love; where there is injury, pardon; where there is doubt, faith; where there is despair, hope; where there is darkness, light; where there is sadness, joy. O Divine Master, grant that I may not so much seek to be consoled, as to console; not so much to be understood as to understand; not so much to be loved as to love: For it is in giving that we receive; it is in pardoning, that we are pardoned; it is in dying, that we awaken to eternal life." —St. Francis of Assisi

What is compassion:

The word compassion means "to have pity (and) a feeling of distress for the ills of others, to suffer with another...to alleviate the consequences of sin or suffering in the lives of others...to moderate one's anger (and) treat with mildness, moderation, and gentleness."[2] Compassion is often described as empathy, benevolence, grace, kindness, mercy, sympathy, understanding or forbearance.

Compassion is a spiritual gift. It is a gift of God to be used for God's glory. In Don and Katie Fortune's biblical handbook to discovering our God-given gifts, the authors discuss the seven motivational gifts listed in Romans 12:6-8. "Of all the gifts, that of compassion is by far the most frequently bestowed."[3] The Fortunes elected to use "compassion" rather than "mercy" for this motivational gift. *To have mercy* in Greek is *eleeo*. *Strong's Exhaustive Concordance of the Bible*[4] defines mercy: "to be compassionate (by word or deed, specifically by divine grace); have compassion, (pity on), have (obtain, receive, shew) mercy (on)."

However, we are not naturally compassionate, even when compassion appears to be our spiritual gift. Compassion is learned by living and by our own experiences. It is developed as we put ourselves into another's shoes, knowing that though we may have had similar life experiences, we cannot know all that the other has or is experiencing.

The Fortunes have identified the following 20 characteristics of the "compassionate person":

- Has tremendous capacity to show love.
- Always looks for good in people.
- Senses the spiritual and emotional atmosphere of a group or individual.
- Is attracted to people who are hurting or in distress.
- Takes action to remove hurts and relieves distress in others.
- Is more concerned for mental and emotional distress than physical distress.
- *Is motivated to help people have right relationships with one another.*
- Loves opportunities to give preference or place to others.
- Takes care with words and actions to avoid hurting others.
- Easily detects insincerity or wrong motives.
- Is drawn to others with the gift of compassion.
- Loves to do thoughtful things for others.
- Is trusting and trustworthy.
- Avoids conflicts and confrontations.
- Does not like to be rushed in a job or activity.
- Is typically cheerful and joyful.
- Is ruled by the heart rather than the head.
- Rejoices to see others blessed and grieves to see others hurt.
- Is a crusader for good causes.
- Intercedes for the hurts and problems of others.

Prerequisites for showing compassion:

The bridge of compassion embraces both a heart saddened by the plight of others as well as doing something about their plight. Before we can exercise compassion, we must see another's woundedness and be moved by it.

Parables and people of compassion in the scriptures:

The story Jesus told of the prodigal son (Luke 15:11-31) illustrates the compassion of a father's heart. Although the father loved both sons equally, he showed compassion to the one who needed it. We do not show compassion because it is deserved. Compassion is undeserved and unearned. The father in this story showed compassion out of love and because doing so was the right thing to do. Showing compassion models our heavenly Father's love for us.

It may be easy to show compassion to those we love, but compassion may be difficult to offer to strangers or to those with whom we may feel some type of bias or discomfort. The parable of the Good Samaritan (Luke 10: 29-37) is a classic example of showing unconditional compassion. The Good Samaritan took pity on a man he did not even know. He made himself available even though he, himself, was, as a Samaritan, considered a despised man. He not only took care of the victim's immediate physical suffering, he also anticipated his on-going emotional and physical needs by providing money for his care. The Good Samaritan had great capacity for love, was drawn to the hurting, responded from the heart, empathized, took action to remove hurt, and through his thoughtful actions removed the potential for further emotional distress. That is *compassion*. Even though the two men would never officially meet, a lasting relationship was birthed through one man's compassion.

Isaiah predicted that the Messiah would heal the brokenhearted and proclaim freedom for spiritual captives and prisoners (Isaiah 61:1-2). Early in his ministry, Jesus proclaimed his purpose: seeking out the lost and restoring them to *relationship* with the Father. He quotes Isaiah (Luke 4: 18-19) to restate his purpose: showing compassion through healing, teaching, ministering, and serving.

In Jeremiah we see God's compassion for His people symbolized in the compassion of the Evil-Merodach, king of Babylon toward Jehoiachin (Jeremiah 52:31-32). Evil-Merodach released Jehoiachin, king of Judah from prison, cared for him and restored him to power. Likewise, the compassion of God would restore the nations of Israel and Judah to their homeland and provide their care.

The restored exiled Israelites knew what it meant to experience God's compassion. Through Zechariah (Zechariah 7:8-10), God instructed them to show mercy and compassion to each other as had He.

The New Testament doctor, Luke, was a physician, historian and traveling companion. Although we know few details of his life, we know that he not only wrote about Jesus Christ's compassion but that he also reflected his Lord's compassion.

In two other New Testament passages the Apostle Paul's compassion is evident. After establishing the church at Thessalonica, Paul was concerned for this young congregation's well-being and sent young Timothy to check out their situation and to encourage the new believers (I Thessalonians 3:2). Even late in his ministry, as a shipwrecked prisoner, Paul continued to show compassion to others. While on Malta, Paul laid hands on, prayed for and healed his host's ill father (Acts 28:7-10).

How to demonstrate compassion:

Simply put, demonstrating compassion requires that we *get involved*, *reach out*, and *risk*. The New Testament writer James reinforces the role of compassion in authentic Christianity:
> What good is it, my brothers, if a man claims to have faith but has no deeds? Can such faith save him? Suppose a brother or sister is without clothes and daily food. If one of you say to him, "Go, I wish you well; keep warm and well fed," but does nothing about his physical needs, what good is it? In the same

way, faith by itself, if it is not accompanied by action, is dead.
James 2: 14-17

Christ reminds us the compassion we show others we are actually showing Him (Matthew 25: 40).

The first step in demonstrating compassion is to see every person as God's creation and to be willing to be available when a need arises. Compassionate people reach out because they sense needs. Most needs are not obvious. If our hearts are available, God will show us the needs. He will also show us how to respond.

Dr. David Stevens, Executive Director of the Christian Medical Association, addressing the role of compassion in medicine states, "There are many times in the practice of medicine when we cannot afford to let our patients' emotions or suffering dissuade us from the treatment they need. Being cool, calm, and objective is important for a doctor; I don't want to minimize that. But at the same time, what patients are looking for, and what they also need, is someone who truly cares about them and demonstrates it. I would go so far as to say that, in my experience, the caring is ultimately more important than the curing—and often may have the greater therapeutic effect."[5] Dr. Stevens shares the practical ways to demonstrate compassion that he talks about to the Christian doctors he works with. The first requirement in demonstrating compassion is *touch*. Second, being compassionate requires a *willingness to invest time*. After touch and time is *temperament*. Temperament covers a lot of territory—speaking directly to and not just about; speaking calmly and using the patient's name, and incorporating humor. Nothing demonstrates a caring temperament better than availability. Finally, Dr. Stevens reminds us that "these same principles can be applied to all our relationships with other people. Our touch, time, and temperament can communicate compassion and caring in our friendship, family, and business relationships alike."

The Bridge of Compassion

Scriptural Insights:

The focus of these scriptural references is to give you a biblical understanding of the Bridge of Compassion. (Scriptures are printed in the back of the book.)

1. *Isa 56: 6-12.*
Summarize the compelling points this Old Testament passage makes about compassion.

2. *Dt 30:3; Dt 32:36; Ne 9:17; Ps 51:1; Ps 86:15; Ps 103:13; Ps 119:156; Ps 145:9; Isa 30:18; Isa 54:10; La 3:22-23; Mic 7:18-19; 2 Co 1:3; Jas 5:11.*
What do we learn about God's compassion from these verses?

3. *Mt 9:35-37; Mt 14: 13-14.*
What characteristics of compassion does Jesus model in these passages?

4. *Pr 14:21; Zec 7:9-10; Mt 7:12; Lk 6:35; Gal 6:2; Eph 4:32; Col 3:12-13.*
What instructions regarding showing compassion are we given in these passages?

5. *Mt 25: 35,40.*
What is the primary evidence to Christ that we are practicing compassion?

6. *Mt. 8:1-4; Mt 9: 27-31; Mk 8:22-26.*
What role does *touch* play in the showing of compassion?

The Bridge of Compassion

Focused Application:

I. Read the story of the paralytic in Mark 2:1-12 (Luke 5:17-26; Matthew 9:1-8). This story shows the role of compassionate friends in the life of the paralytic.

    a. Describe a time in your life when you needed physical, emotional and/or spiritual help and a compassionate person came alongside you and met your need.

    b. Describe a time in your life when you have recognized a physical, emotional or spiritual need in someone whom you then comforted.

II. Refer back to Don and Katie Fortune's characteristics of the compassion person in "Core Concepts". Which of these characteristics describe you?

III. How do you rate your compassion quotient?

    0_____10

IV. Are you more effective at recognizing persons who need compassion, showing compassion, or both? Explain.

V. How well do you employ each of Dr. David Stevens' requirements for demonstrating compassion?

TOUCH

0_____10

TIME

0_____10

TEMPERAMENT

0_____10

VI. What proactive compassionate behaviors will you commit to beginning?

CHAPTER 5

The Bridge of Contentment

Key Scripture: But godliness with contentment is great gain. I Timothy 6:6

Overview:
God created us to be in *relationship* with Him. He wants the complete desire of our souls to be satisfied by Him. In the core of our souls, do we *experience* God? Do we *feel* God? Do we *enjoy* God? Do we drink until the thirst to relate to God is satisfied?

The Contentment Bridge study guide addresses the following:

- What true contentment is.
- What contentment is not.
- Biblical examples of contentment
- God's plan for our true contentment

Scriptural references throughout provide Biblical support for the bridge.

The "Focused Application" segment allows you to apply the scriptural principles addressed in "Core Concepts" and "Scriptural Insights".

Core concepts:
"I doubt if anyone who has tasted joy would ever, if both were in his power, exchange it for all the pleasures in the world." —C.S. Lewis

In the Old Testament, peace is described as security (Ps 4:8), *contentment* (Is. 26:3), prosperity (Ps. 122:6-7), and the absence of war (I Sam. 7:14)

In the New Testament, Jesus speaks of a peace that brings a quietness to the mind and soul through reconciliation with God (i.e. being in *relationship* with God). Such peace was proclaimed:
- By the host of angels at Christ's birth (Luke 2:14)
- By Christ himself in the Sermon on the Mount (Matt. 5:9) and throughout his ministry.
- Through the Lord's Supper, shortly before Christ's death (John 14:27).
- By the apostle Paul who later wrote that such peace (spiritual contentment) is experienced through faith in Christ (Rom.5:1)

What true contentment is:

Contentment involves desiring God so passionately "that every other desire and every circumstance, positive or negative, can be fully felt without being controlled by them."[1] It is having a hope that thrives when dreams come true and when dreams are shattered. Happiness is not found in a certain set of circumstances but rather in a certain set of attitudes.

The desire to be happy, to be content, ought not prompt apology. Our souls were designed to be content, to be at peace. They long for whatever we think will provide the greatest pleasure. Most often we are not aware that an intimate relationship with God IS that greatest pleasure, that it is true contentment.[2]

Paul knew how to be content whether he had plenty or was in need (Philippians 4:11-12). The secret was being in *relationship* with Christ and drawing on His power for strength. Paul was content because he could see life from God's point of view. He focused on what he was suppose to do, not what he felt he should have. Paul had his priorities straight. He had detached himself from the non-essentials so he could concentrate on the eternal.

What contentment is not:

We need God. He is all we need. However, until we realize that fact, we experience lesser desires as needs and devote our energy to arranging for their satisfaction. That defines addiction. When the deepest desire of our heart is something other than God, a spirit of entitlement develops. We reach for whatever brings satisfaction, relieves pain for the moment, and we thereby create deeper emptiness that rudely clamors for relief.[3]

We are thirsty people. We long for (1) physical comfort (casual longings), (2) good relationship with people (critical longings), and (3) the contentment that only a relationship with God provides (crucial longings). Christ has not promised to meet either our casual or critical longings. We may therefore bump into some hard times with material problems and unrewarding relationships. God will instead faithfully provide all we need to accomplish His purpose in us and through us. He has promised to satisfy our crucial longings, but (a) the satisfaction is only a taste; the banquet comes later, and (b) the satisfaction of crucial longings does not dull the pain of disappointment when our casual and critical longings go unmet.[4]

Frequently we expect "more" will bring contentment. Often the desire for "more" is really a longing to fill an empty space in one's life. To what are you drawn when you feel thirsty or empty? How can you find *contentment*? The answer lies in your priorities, your perspective, and your source of power.

Biblical examples of contentment:

When Paul wrote Philippians, he was in a Roman prison waiting to hear if he would be executed. Yet we hear no whining or complaining. Instead, he learned to accept the circumstances he could not change. Even under house arrest, Paul experienced the peace and contentment that come only by being in relationship with God and following His will. Paul used his time in prison to carry the message of salvation to people in need. "For two whole years Paul stayed in Rome in his own rented house and welcomed all who came to see him. Boldly and without hindrance he preached the kingdom of God and taught about the Lord Jesus Christ" (Acts 28:30-31). The apostle's life is an example to each of us, showing the importance and benefits of persisting in our *relationship* with God and sharing our faith.

John the Baptist is another biblical example of contentment (Luke 7:24-28). Because of his strength of character, John the Baptist did not allow himself to be squeezed into anyone else's mold. Rather, he committed himself to fulfill his role as a prophet and forerunner of the Messiah. He knew the boundaries of his role and fulfilled his God-given purpose.

God's plan for our true contentment:

God has a purpose for each of us. As we discover our role in His plan, following the vision He gives us will bring us contentment. As we follow His will, He will always be with us, guiding and strengthening us along the way. Trying to be someone we were never intended to be only slows our spiritual growth and contentment.

Life is not fair. It is not predictable or controllable. It can be wonderfully rich in some ways and terribly difficult in others. When we are willing to face the hurts in our life and consider how we have reacted to them, then our discomfort can lead us to *contentment*. "God grant me the serenity to accept the things I cannot change, the courage to change the things I can and the wisdom to know the difference" (The Serenity Prayer).

The four chapters of Paul's letter to the Philippians pictures four facets of contentment:

Chapter 1: For contented living, I need the right role model, Jesus Christ (1:21)

Chapter 2: To serve with contentment, I need the right attitude—Christ's attitude (2:5)

Chapter 3: For sharing a contented life, I need an eternal goal, "the upward call of God in Christ Jesus" (3:14)

Chapter 4: For contented rest, I need the peace that comes through laying my needs before Christ (4:6-7)

How many truly contented people do you know? As the apostle Paul said, "I have *learned* to be content, whatever the circumstances may be" (Phil 4:11). Contentment is a trait to be learned through practice and diligence. Tim Hansel suggests "Four Commandments of Contentment":[5]

1. *Thou shalt live here and now.*

Life, God's life within us, is happening here and now. The paradox is that we must practice the presence; otherwise, it will elude us. We are sitting on a miracle, but we do not recognize it. God has given us everything we need to be happy.

We have the idea that God is leading us to a desired goal. He is not. God's training is for now. God's end is to enable me to see that he can work in the chaos of my life right now. God is not only the God of history and of the future, but also very much the God of the now, the God of the process.

2. *Thou shalt not hurry.*

Our world seems intoxicated with hurry. One of the greatest sins of this age may be hurry. For in our impatient desire to make things happen, we have, inadvertently, overlooked what is really important.

3. *Thou shalt not take thyself too seriously.*

    The tragic result of taking ourselves too seriously is that in our fear of becoming childlike, in our fear of becoming a fool for Christ, in our fear of being seen as we are, we discover all too late that it is impossible to be fully human and fully alive without Christ.

4. *Thou shalt be grateful.*

    "Give thanks in all circumstances; for this is God's will for you in Christ Jesus "(1 Thess. 5:18). Gratitude is not an option for a Christian. Gratitude is the source of peace and contentment.

The Bridge of Contentment

Scriptural Insights:

The focus of these scriptural references is to give you a biblical understanding of the Bridge of Contentment. (Scriptures are printed in the back of the book.)

1. I Tim. 6:6-9; Heb 13:5-6; Ecc 4:8; Luke 12:22-31; Mt. 6:25-33
What do these verses tell us about the relationship between materialism and contentment?

2. Job 36:11-12; Pr. 19:23; Isa 26:3; Lev. 18:4-5*
What do these verses tell us about the relationship between obedience and contentment?
Note: the Hebrew expression "to live" in this passage does not just mean "to exist". It refers to finding contentment and enjoyment in life—living life to its fullest.

3. Ps 63:1-5
According to this psalm, what does man earnestly seek and thirst for?

Relationship

4. *Num. 6:24-26*
What is God's desire for all of His people according to this passage?

5. *Phil 4:11-12; Num. 27:12-23.*
What do we learn about being content regardless of our circumstances from these verses?

6. *Pr. 15:17; 17:1 and 16:8.*
What did King Solomon have to say about contentment? Note the three comparative couplets above. In each the former things named are better than the latter.

7. *Ecc 5:18-20.*
Contentment and material blessing don't have to be mutually exclusive. What do these words from King Solomon say to concur with this?
Note: The focus of this passage is on gladness of the heart rather than on wealth, possessions, or work, all of which are provided by God.

8. 2 Pe 1:3-9
What keys to living a contented life are found in this passage?

9. The Book of Philippians
The heart of Paul's letter to the Philippians is contentment. He did not write to answer any profound questions or to solve sticky problems or even to deal with a particular sin. Instead, he wrote to express joy and encourage contentment in dear friends. As you read this epistle, look for the following:

Chapter 1 opens with Paul's cheerful admission that his prayers for the Philippians bring joy to his heart.

In Chapter 2 Paul encourages the Philippians to work together in harmony. By doing so enriches his own joy.

In Chapter 3 Paul reminds the Philippians to find their contentment and joy in the Lord.

In Chapter 4 Paul repeats the command of Chapter 3. He reminds the Philippians to think upon that which leads to contentment. Lastly, Paul mentions the great joy he feels due to the Philippians' care and concern for him.

Relationship

Focused Application:

I. The Plague of Discontentment

Do you suffer from the contagious plague of discontment? It's more affectionately referred to as the "If Only" disease!!

- If only I had a better job
- If only I had more money
- If only I had a bigger house
- If only I could lose 10 pounds
- If only I were a better student
- If only I had made better investments
- If only I had married—
- If only my marriage was more fulfilling
- If only we could take a vacation
- If only we could communicate better
- If only we could have children
- If only we didn't have so many children
- If only the kids were more well behaved
- If only my parents hadn't divorced
- If only my business could have succeeded
- If only I had more friends
- If only my husband/wife didn't have cancer

The list is endless.
Read through the "if only" list. Which "if onlys" apply to you?

What "if onlys" are missing?

What do you need to do to transform your "if only" discontents into contentment?

The Bridge of Contentment

II. In the "Core Concepts", the four facets of contentment which are described in Philippians were identified. Now let us rate how you are doing in these four areas on a ten point scale (10 high):

Contentment in living: 1 2 3 4 5 6 7 8 9 10

Contentment in serving: 1 2 3 4 5 6 7 8 9 10

Contentment in sharing: 1 2 3 4 5 6 7 8 9 10

Contentment in resting: 1 2 3 4 5 6 7 8 9 10

Which area of contentment did you rate highest? Lowest? Why?

III. "Restore to me the joy of your salvation and grant me a willing spirit to sustain me."
$$\text{Psalm 51:12}$$

God wants me to have joy and contentment, because they enable me to _____

IV. "But let all who take refuge in you be glad;
let them ever sing for joy.
Spread your protection over them,
that those who love your name may rejoice in you."
Ps 5:11

What does having God in your life help you overcome?

> "We can tell from our experience that His light is more powerful than the deepest darkness—How wonderful that the reality of His presence is greater than the reality of the hell about us."
> —Betsie ten Boom, to her sister, Corrie

Relationship

I want to overcome _____ and replace it with contentment.

V. Practical Suggestions for Contentment

1. Do not play roles. Trying to be someone you are not, only creates discontent.
2. Choose your friends wisely. Associate with those who encourage and edify you from a godly perspective.
3. Do not let things drift. If you have a problem, seek godly wisdom for a plan or solution.
4. Admit your fears. Find out what frightens you and try to determine why.
5. Make time to get away, to mediate, to relax and relate with the Lord.
6. Do something for others. There is contentment in serving.
7. Be willing to compromise. Let your motto be "do it God's way, not mine."
8. Work on a realistic self-image. Look in the mirror; you are created in God's image.
9. Always do what is right. The contentment of integrity has no substitute.
10. Take one thing at a time. Distress and contentment do not mix.
11. Seek balance in your life. Invite the Lord into your work and leisure.
12. Be realistic. Life has its ups and downs.
13. Avoid excuses. Be proactive. Claim peace today, not someday.
14. Talk things over with the Lord, a friend, a relative, a pastor or a counselor.

CHAPTER 6

The Bridge of Forgiveness

Key Scripture: Bear with each other and forgive whatever grievances you may have against one another. Forgive as the Lord forgave you. Colossians 3:13

Overview:
Relationship with God begins through forgiveness. Jesus Christ went to the cross for our forgiveness. As Christians we are commanded in God's word to forgive one another. To enjoy relationship with others, we must learn to forgive.

The "Bridge of Forgiveness" study guide addresses the following:
- Christ's example of forgiveness
- Learning to release others through forgiveness
- What forgiveness is not
- What forgiveness is
- Rejecting bitterness as a way of life
- The role of humility in forgiveness

Scriptural references throughout provide biblical support for the bridge.

The "Focused Application" segment allows you to apply the scriptural principles addressed in "Core Concepts" and "Scriptural

Insights".

Core Concepts:

While the pain someone has inflicted on you is real, it is also negligible compared to the wrong you have committed against God. The difference between another person's sin against you and your sin against God is the difference between $16.00 and $5,000,000.00 Forgiveness is the obligation of the forgiven.[1]

Christ's Example of Forgiveness:

Then Jesus said, "Father, forgive them, for they do not know what they do" (John 23:34). In this text Jesus is forgiving his tormentors, both Jews and Romans. Jesus went on to say, "for they do not know what they do." They were not aware of the full scope of their wickedness. They did not recognize Him as the true Messiah. These people were blind to the light of divine truth. Their ignorance, however, did not mean that they deserved forgiveness. But Christ's prayer while they were in the very act of mocking Him is an expression of the boundless compassion of divine forgiveness. Jesus, during His own crucifixion, the most painful and disgraceful form of execution the Romans employed, was still forgiving.

> For to this you were called, because Christ also suffered for us, leaving us an example, that you should follow His steps: 'Who committed no sin, nor was deceit found in His mouth', who when He was reviled, did not revile in return; when he suffered, He did not threaten, but committed Himself to Him who judges righteously; who Himself bore our sins in His own body on the cross, that we having died to sins, might live for righteousness—by whose stripes you were healed. For you were like sheep going astray, but have now returned to the Shepherd and Overseer of your souls. (1 Peter 2:21-25)

For those of us called to salvation in Christ, we are patiently enduring. Peter's point is that a person called to salvation will, sometimes at least, have to endure unfair treatment. This is especially true in relationships. Commendable behavior on the part of the believer in the midst of such trials results in the strengthening and perfecting of the Christian's life. Forgiveness is a way of glorifying God. Christ is the pattern for Christians to follow in suffering with perfect patience. His death was primarily for the atonement for sin, but it was also exemplary, as a model of endurance in unjust suffering. We see in I Peter 2:23, though reviled or verbally abused, Christ never retaliated with vicious words and threats. Christ handed himself over to such suffering because of His perfect confidence in the sovereignty and righteousness of His Father.

Christ suffered not simply as the Christian's pattern, but far more importantly as the Christian's substitute. To bear sins was to be punished for them. Christ bore the punishment and the penalty for believers, thus satisfying a holy God. The great doctrine of the substitutionary atonement is the heart of the gospel. We have been declared righteous, through God's forgiveness; we can walk in newness of life. Through the wounds of Christ at the cross, believers are healed spiritually from the disease of sin. We see through this section of scripture that Christ is the Christian's standard. As the Christian journeys daily back to the cross, human relationships are transformed into divine interactions. Jesus stands between you and God, bringing two who were estranged together into a loving relationship. Jesus stands between you and others, handing you the opportunity to live beyond self in love and forgiveness.

Learning to Release Others Through Forgiveness:
  What Forgiveness Is Not:

> Forgiveness is not a cover up or a game of 'let's pretend'. It is not a performance in which we shrug our shoulders and pretend the offense was 'no big deal'. Forgiveness is not teeth-gritting determination to keep going no matter what. Sheer willpower to overlook or minimize an offense will never achieve forgiveness. Quite often, such an approach creates bitterness instead, especially when the other person fails to respond as desired. Forgiveness is not a passive resolve to wait the problem out, hoping

time will heal all wounds. Forgiveness is not merely excusing people who offend our personal preferences or who annoy us by their selfish choices, such as a friend who orders a pizza with everything on it when he knows you don't eat olives and mushrooms, or the obnoxious driver who cuts you off the freeway during your rush-hour commute. These may test our tolerance levels, but not our willingness to forgive.[2]

What Forgiveness Is:

Forgiveness releases a legitimate debt. There are things we rightfully owe people. We owe love to God others and our enemies according to the scriptures. We owe honor not only to our parents, but to others as well. We owe obedience to God, and to those in authority. While we know how we should treat others and how we want them to treat us, we still fail. Sometimes these failures badly wound us or we badly wound others. Christ has set the example to forgive and He commands us to forgive. This is extremely difficult because we have been violated. He knows He is speaking to people whose trust has been shattered, whose character has been unjustly damaged and whose lives have been marred by the sin of others. In the midst of all this pain and disillusionment, Christ says, forgive.

Christ never minimizes the violations that damage lives. He never suggests the offense and its harm are not to be taken seriously. We are told by Christ to release the legitimate debt. When we forgive, we guarantee that the offending person's violation will not be held against him.

Regardless of the failed obligation or violation, Jesus says, "Forgive". To silence all exception, He says, "as I have forgiven you." We can not debate; there is no argument. We owe Christ our total obedience. He has paid the debt for all our sins. We are forgiven, therefore we are to forgive others.

Forgiveness goes against all natural inclinations for immediate personal justice. Ourselves are set aside; the focus becomes Christ. Regardless of how horrible the pain, the wounds, the injustices, and the utter sorrow, we must view the person from the cross. True forgiveness comes from trusting in Christ and the values of His kingdom.[2]

Rejecting Bitterness as a Way of Life:

The blight of bitterness may be doing a number on your life. Bitterness can be exposed through animosity, grudge, resentment, and faultfinding. These things indicate a refusal to release an offender from payment for a perceived offense. Most people learn to accept their bitterness. The Bible sternly warns about a "root of bitterness". "See to it that no one misses the grace of God, and that no bitter root grows up to cause trouble, and defile many" (Hebrews 12:15).

"What is a 'bitter root'? A bitter root starts with a real or imagined offense brought on by another. It comes in various forms:
- Your character is assassinated.
- You are unjustly fired from your job.
- You are falsely accused of something you did not do.
- You are cheated out of an inheritance.
- You were robbed.
- You were raped.
- You were made fun of by someone else.
- Someone made a racial slur against you.
- You were cheated on by your spouse.

Such a list could go on for pages, but one thing is for sure. People wronged by others often feel it is their God-given right and duty to even the score. The problem, however, is that even after someone feels he or she has finally evened the score, the root of bitterness inside does not go away.[3]

Holding on to bitterness puts us in bondage. The person we fail to forgive remains in control of a segment of our lives. Bitterness interrupts our worship to God, blocks our prayers, lessens our lives for God and assumes we have a right to be unforgiving. By simply allowing God to be God and walking obediently because we love Him and believe His word to be truth, we can reject bitterness as a way of life. It is ultimately our decision to make.

The Role of Humility in Forgiveness:

To forgive, one must be willing to confess to God that he is sinning by harboring bitterness. This takes humility. Admitting to an accountability person your struggle with forgiveness requires humility. It certainly involves humbleness to go to someone and forgive them. To build relationships God's way requires loving unconditionally. To love is to take an incredible risk. Humility does not make sense in human terms, but if we are in Christ, we will choose "Kingdom Principles". This will create a freedom to relate deeply with God and man.

Scriptural Insights:

The focus of these scriptural references is to give you a biblical understanding of the "Bridge of Forgiveness". (Scriptures are printed in the back of the book.)

1. Luke 6:36; Ephesians 4: 31-32; Matthew 18:35; Mark 11:25-26; Matthew 6:14; 2 Corinthians 2:10-11
What reasons do these verses give for the need to forgive others?

2. Luke 17:3
How many instructions regarding forgiveness does this verse provide?

3. Matthew 18:21-23
According to these verses, how many times are we to forgive?

4. Romans 12:19; Proverbs 20:22
According to these verses, whose responsibility is revenge?

5. Colossians 1:14
Who is the role model of forgiveness?

6. Genesis 33:1-11
What does this reunion of two brothers teach us about ridding our lives of bitterness?

7. Philippians 1:12-14
What does Paul teach us about turning bitterness into opportunity?

8. Hebrews 12:15
What are the dangers of bitterness?

Focused Application:

I. Are you practicing the three R's of forgiveness?

    a. Do you <u>remember</u> daily the forgiveness you have in Christ?

        never   seldom   sometimes   almost always   always

    b. Are you <u>releasing</u> people of the sins they have committed against you?

        never   seldom   sometimes   almost always   always

    c. Are you rejecting the temptation to pick back up the offense someone has done against you?

        never   seldom   sometimes   almost always   always

II. Are you currently going through a situation where you are being called to forgive someone? If yes, are you responding obediently?

III. Is your fellowship with God being affected by your measure of forgiveness toward others? How?

IV. Are you ready to confess and turn from your bitterness?

What may be getting in the way of you following through?

V. How have you felt in the past when you have forgiven your offender?

Relationship

VI. Are you currently loving others the way Christ commanded us to love?

What step can you take this week toward getting yourself in alignment with God's word?

VII. Are you being honest about the bitterness that is being harbored toward someone?

VIII. Pray right now for the Holy Spirit to empower you to live freely in Christ as you practice forgiveness.

CHAPTER 7

The Bridge of Grace

Key Scripture: Every good gift and every perfect gift is from above, and comes down from the Father of lights, with whom there is no variation or shadow of turning. James 1:17

Overview:
Two different Greek words for gift emphasize the perfection and inclusiveness of God's graciousness. The first denotes the act of giving, and the second is the object given. Everything related to divine giving is adequate, complete and beneficial. In John 3:27, Jesus said, "A man can receive nothing unless it has been given to him from heaven." Grace is such a divine gift to be enjoyed and given away to others. God has given us all that we need to experience relationship with Him and others. Grace is such a significant building stone in successful relating. We all want to be accepted, loved and appreciated. The way to give this to others and the way to receive this from others is through grace.

The "Bridge of Grace" study guide addresses the following:

- What true grace is.
- How a need for control interrupts the flow of grace
- Biblical examples of grace

Scriptural references throughout provide biblical support for the bridge.

The "Focused Application" segment allows you to apply the scriptural principles addressed in "Core Concepts" and "Scriptural Insights".

Core Concepts:

"God does well in giving the grace of consolation, but man does evil in not returning everything gratefully to God. Thus, the gifts of grace cannot flow in us when we are ungrateful to the Giver, when we do not return them to the Fountainhead. Grace is always given to him who is duly grateful, and what is wont to be given the humble will be taken away from the proud." Thomas A Kempis [1]

In the Old Testament, we read "I will pour on the house of David and on the inhabitants of Jerusalem the Spirit of grace and supplication; then they will look on Me whom they pierced..." (Zechariah 12:10). In Zechariah 4:7, we find the words, "Grace, grace to it!" This blessing signifying shouts of joy and thanksgiving came to pass over the completion of the temple.

In the New Testament, grace is described:
    as great (Acts 4:33)
    as sovereign (Romans 5:21)
    as rich (Ephesians 1:7)
    as exceeding (2 Corinthians 9:14)
    as all-sufficient (2 Corinthians 12:9)
    as all-abundant (Romans 5:15, 17, 20)
    as glorious (Ephesians 1:6)

What true grace is:

Grace is a supernatural ability given directly from God. We must be recipients of His grace in order to become conduits of His grace. Grace is the unmerited favor of God toward sinful humanity. When we begin to capture the awesomeness of this reality, we become more gracious toward others. Max Lucado says it well in his book,

In The Grip of Grace: "Where the grace of God is missed, bitterness is born. But where the grace of God is embraced, forgiveness flourishes. The longer we walk in the garden, the more likely we are to smell like flowers. The more we immerse ourselves in grace, the more likely we are to give grace."[2] With this quote, the picture begins to become clearer. Grace is a gift from God. We must receive the gift in order to be able to give it to others.

The apostle Paul understood that it is God who makes people right through faith in Jesus Christ. This is clearly a work of grace. Grace is exercising a reality we cling to by faith. To exercise this reality, we see others as we see ourselves, as poor, pitiful, helpless people in need of grace. Grace is extending love, forgiveness and acceptance even when we do not feel like it or see the possibility of doing so. Grace is living life in such an attitude of thanksgiving to God for His indescribable gift to us that it brims over the edges of our lives onto others. Grace is believing that nothing can separate us from the love of God that is in Christ Jesus (Romans 8:35).

How a need for control interrupts the flow of grace in our relationships:

There are three glaring reasons why the issue of control interrupts the flow of grace in our relationships. First, man is unable to comprehend the truth of God or grasp His standard of righteousness. Sadly this spiritual ignorance does not result from a lack of opportunity, but is an expression of his depravity and rebellion. Our natural tendency is to seek our own interests. All of us are inclined to leave God's way and pursue our own. Therefore, we attempt to control others by imposing harsh expectations or subtle forms of manipulation. The root issue is the inability to get past ourselves.

The second reason control interrupts the flow of grace in relationships is based upon our life experiences. Living in a fallen world, full of fallen people, produces wounded people. We have all been wounded. Words can be said, actions can be taken toward us, a look, a gesture, can evoke the horror of memories of past painful experiences. Because of this reality, we all attempt to self-protect

Relationship

by being the controller in relationships. Obviously, we do not want the pain from the past to complicate our current relationships. Therefore, we base our relational strategies upon our experiences rather than our new identity in Christ and the fact that we can be set free from our past. We are generally more committed to self-protection than moving toward each other in ways that would please God.

The third reaction leading to control is that grace seems unfair. Why should I love, forgive or accept you, when I have not been loved or forgiven or accepted? The attitude seems to be, "I am not going to make myself vulnerable to you. You could really harm me; therefore I am going to control our relationship." To unregenerate people or to the carnal Christians, grace will not make sense. The overwhelming need for control will dominate all of their relationships.

Biblical examples of Grace:

"God shows his great love for us in this way: Christ died for us while we were still sinners" (Romans 5:8).

Have you ever been given a place of honor at a banquet table? Has anyone ever cooked a meal for you? It is very humbling to know you are an imperfect human being and someone is honoring you. Christ welcomes us to his table by virtue of his love and our request. It is not our offerings that grant us a place at the feast; indeed, anything we bring appears puny at his table. Our admission of hunger is the only demand, for "Blessed are those who hunger and thirst for righteousness, for they shall be filled" (Matthew 5:6). Our hunger, then, is not a longing to be avoided but rather a God-given desire to be heeded.

In Luke 15:11-31, we read yet another marvelous illustration of grace. In this story we find a father with two sons. The prodigal son evidently took his share in liquid assets and left, abandoning his father, and heading into a life of iniquity, not merely wasteful extravagance, but also wanton immorality. The Greek word for "prodigal" means dissolute and conveys the idea of an utterly debauched lifestyle. When the son came to his senses and decided to come back home, the father was there, looking and waiting. This is an excellent illustration of God's grace toward us. The father's eagerness and joy at his son's return is unmistakable. The father is not indifferent or hostile, but a Savior by nature, longing to forgive the wayward son.

Relationship

Scriptural Insights:

The focus of these scriptural references is to give you a biblical understanding of the Bridge of Grace. (Scriptures are printed in the back of the book.)

1. *Romans 3:21-22, Romans 4:5, 2 Cor. 5:19,21*
How do you see yourself, if you are in Christ?

2. *1 Jn 4:10, Col. 2:14*
To what extent does God love you?

3. *Romans 5:1-3, Eph. 3:12, Ps. 36:5, Ps. 103: 9-14*
Are you enjoying God's grace in your life?

4. *Rom. 8:1, Eph. 2:13, Col. 1:13, Heb. 13:5, Eph 2:18*
What do these verses say about your relationship with God?

5. *2 Cor 12:7-9*
What does this passage say about grace?

6. Matt. 18:21-35, Eph. 4:32, 2 Tim. 2:1
How are we to relate to each other?

7. Rom. 8:31-39
According to the above scriptures, does grace ever run out?

Focused Application

I. How is a lack of grace in your current relationships affecting them?
Give specific illustrations.

II. What affect is grace having in your current relationships?
Give current results of grace at work, i.e. marriage, parenting, etc.

III. In "Core Concepts" Max Lucado was quoted, "The more we immerse ourselves in grace, the more likely we are to give grace."
    A. Who is the most gracious person you know?
        Describe him or her.

    B. How can we immerse ourselves in grace? What does that mean?

IV. Are you practicing Matthew 18:21-35?

    A. How have you failed to extend grace to someone else?

    B. What keeps you from forgiving?

V. How important is this "Bridge of Grace" in your relationships?

0 _____10

VI. How do your beliefs need to change in regards to God's grace toward you?

How will this affect your extending grace to others?

VII. What is the role of humility in a grace-lived life?

CHAPTER 8

The Bridge of Hope

Key Scripture: "For I know the plans I have for you," declares the Lord, "plans to prosper you and not to harm you, plans to give you hope and a future." —Jeremiah 29:11

Overview:

Christians have a corner on hope. Hope is a relationship with Jesus Christ, the Son of God, who came and who will come again. Hope is the bridge from the past, to the present, to the future. Hope is spiritual optimism.

The "Bridge of Hope" study guide addresses the following:
- What hope is and is not
- Benefits of hope
- How we develop hope
- The importance of sharing hope

Scriptural references throughout provide biblical support for the bridge.

The "Focused Application" segment allows you to apply the scriptural principles addressed in "Core Concepts" and "Scriptural Insights".

Core concepts:

"Hope is one of the Theological virtues. This means that a continual looking forward to the eternal world is not (as some modern people think) a form of escapism or wishful thinking, but one of the things a Christian is meant to do. It does not mean that we are to leave the present world as it is. If you read history you will find that the Christians who did most for the present world were just those who thought most of the next. The Apostles themselves, who set on foot the conversion of the Roman Empire, the great men who built up the Middle Ages, the English Evangelicals who abolished the Slave Trade, all left their mark on Earth, precisely because their minds were occupied with Heaven. It is since Christians have largely ceased to think of the other world that they have become so ineffective in this. Aim at Heaven and you will get Earth 'thrown in': aim at Earth and you will get neither." —C. S. Lewis [1]

What hope is and is not:

"The word hope I take for faith; and indeed hope is nothing else but the constancy of faith." —John Calvin

Hope is anticipating, awaiting, believing, and being sure of, cherishing, counting on, depending on, contemplating, expecting, and feeling confident of; hope is having faith. By definition, hope is a future reality. "Who hopes for what he already has?" (Rom. 824b)

"The story of every character God uses in the Bible is the story of hope.
    Hope is what made Abraham leave his home.
    Hope is what made Moses willing to take on Pharaoh.
    Hope is what drove the prophets to keep taking on city hall."[2]

Hope is something inside of us and outside of us.[3] The inside of us hope is a sense of longing mixed with anticipation. Bible writers describe this confident expectation as "the fruit of our suffering" (Ro. 5:4), the basis of our endurance (I Thess. 1:3) and patience (Ps. 33:20), and the source of our joy (Ro. 12:12). It is God's work in us

(Jer. 29:11) but our responsibility to nurture and guard. We are challenged to take hold of (Heb. 6:18), be sure of (Heb. 6:11) and hold unswervingly to (Heb. 10:23 the hope we profess.

The hope outside of us is that sure and certain reality to which our inside hope is pinned." It is hope of "the glorious appearing of our great God and Savior, Jesus Christ" (Titus 2:13). It is also our hope of heaven (Col. 1:5).

Hope is not found in things or circumstances. It is not found in possessions, in our own strength, in our accomplishments, in people's love, in our earthly family tree. The writers of scripture admonish us against putting our hope in anything other than God (Ps. 33:17; 1 Tim. 6:17). Ecclesiastes 1:2 proclaims "Meaningless! Meaningless! Utterly meaningless! Everything is meaningless." King Solomon had tried everything—wisdom, pleasures, folly, toil, possession, and fame—only to declare that life is meaningless outside of God's goodness and control.

The word hopeless need not be part of a believer's vocabulary. Having been crucified with Christ (Gal. 2:20) and being indwelled by the Holy Spirit (Eph. 1: 13-14), we have a guarantee of hope.

Max Lucado sums up what hope is and is not:[4] "Hope is not what you expect; it is what you would never dream. It is a wild, improbable tale with a pinch-me-I'm dreaming ending. It is Abraham adjusting his bifocals so he can see not his grandson, but his son. It is Moses standing in the promised land not with Aaron or Miriam at his side, but with Elijah and the transfigured Christ. It's Zechariah left speechless at the sight of his wife Elizabeth, gray-headed and pregnant. And it is the two Emmaus-bound pilgrims reaching out to take a piece of bread only to see that the hands from which it is offered are pierced.

"Hope is not a granted wish or a favor performed; no, it is far greater than that. It is a zany, unpredictable dependence on a God who loves to surprise us out of our socks and be there in the flesh to see our reaction."

Benefits of hope:

Hope deferred makes the heart sick, but a longing fulfilled is a tree of life. (Pr 13:12)

Throughout Scripture we are reminded of the benefits of hope. Among the many benefits are:
- First and foremost: new birth through the resurrection of Jesus (1 Pe 1:3)
- God's unfailing love (Ps 33:22)
- God's protection (Ps 25:21)
- No shame (Ps 25:3)
- A glad heart (Ps 16:9)
- Happiness (Ps 146:5)
- God's graciousness, compassion and blessing (Isa 30:18)
- Renewed strength; the ability to soar, run and walk (Isa 40:31)
- No fear (Jer 17:7-8)
- Ability to bear fruit (Jer 17:7-8)
- Not consumed (Lam 3:21-22)
- God's ear (Mic 7:7)
- Joy and peace (Ro 15:13)
- God's love shed abroad (Ro 5:3-5)
- The riches of his glorious inheritance in the saints (Eph 1:18)

From the perspective of modern day emotional intelligence, having hope means that one will not give in to overwhelming anxiety, a defeatist attitude, or depression in the face of difficult challenges or setbacks.[5]

In addition to its motivating influence, hope also holds *healing power*. Dr. William Buchholz reports:[6] "As I ate breakfast one morning, I overheard two oncologists conversing. One complained bitterly, 'You know, Bob, I just don't understand it. We used the same drugs, the same dosage, the same schedule and the same entry criteria. Yet I got a 22 percent response rate and you got a 74 percent. That's unheard of for metastatic cancer. How do you do it?' His colleague replied, 'We're both using Etoposide, Platinum, Oncovin and Hydroxyurea. You call yours EPOH. I tell my patients I'm giving them HOPE. As dismal as the statistics are, I emphasize that *we have hope*.'"

How we develop hope:

Hope and *waiting* go hand in hand. "I wait for the Lord, my soul waits, and in his word I put my hope" (Ps 130:5). Waiting and hoping demonstrate our willingness to let God have His way.

When we struggle, when we are in pain, when we are confused, we need to know that we are in relationship with Jesus, the Son of God. Too often we seek to understand and sort through psychological issues and physical concerns rather than to know God. *Understanding* the issues or problems and how they came about does not always help. Getting a focus on God and letting Him shine light on the issues will. *Understanding* can leave us *hopeless;* God brings the *hope*.

Spiritual optimism is a key to hope. David's spiritual optimism as he prepared to fight the giant Goliath illustrates the importance the knowledge that God is with us gives. "Then David said to the Philistine, 'You come to me with a sword, with a spear, and with a javelin. But I come to you in the name of the Lord of hosts, the God of the armies of Israel, whom you have defied. This day the Lord will deliver you into my hand" (1 Sam. 17:45-46a). David's assurance of God's presence, this powerful hope, prevented him from becoming discouraged. It is impossible to stand in the presence of God and be a pessimist.

Peter's request to come to Jesus on the Sea of Galilee (Mt. 14:28) illustrates the role of *focusing on Jesus* in the development of hope. While Peter's mind was focused on Jesus, he was empowered to walk on the water. But when his focus was on the storm, his fear short-circuited his ability to receive God's sustaining power.[7]

"Our ability to live in hope to remain focused on Christ during the storm is largely dependent on *what we feed our minds.* This is how we are able to focus on the Savior rather than the storm."[8] The following story illustrates what a mind focused on hope looks like: A church woman recently diagnosed with cancer was given three months to live. Her doctor told her to make preparations to die, so she contacted her pastor and told him how she wanted things arranged for her funeral service-which songs she wanted to have sung, what Scriptures should be read, what words should be spoken-and that she wanted to be buried with her favorite Bible.

But before he left, she called out to him, "One more thing." "What?" "This is important. I want to be buried with a fork in my right hand."

The pastor did not know what to say. No one had ever made such a request before. So she explained. "In all my years going to church functions, whenever food was involved, my favorite part was when whoever was cleaning dishes of the main course would lean over and say, *You can keep your fork.*

"It was my favorite part because I knew that it meant something great was coming. It wasn't Jell-O. It was something with substance—cake or pie—biblical food.

"So I just want people to see me there in my casket with a fork in my hand, and I want them to wonder, *What's with the fork?* Then I want you to tell them, *Something better is coming. Keep your fork.*"

The pastor hugged the woman good-bye. And soon after, she died.

At the funeral service people saw the dress she had chosen, saw the Bible she loved, and heard the songs she loved, but they all asked the same question: "What's with the fork?"

The pastor explained that this woman, their friend, wanted them to know that for her-or for anyone who dies in Christ—this is not a day of defeat. It is a day of celebration. The real party is just starting.

Something better is coming.

So this week why not make the humble fork your own personal icon? Each time you sit down to a meal, take a look at the utensil on the left of your plate, and remember the woman who took one to her casket. When you pause to give thanks for the food, give thanks for your *hope* as well. Each time you wrap your fingers around the handle of a fork, remember: "Something better is coming."
—Author unknown.

Finally, *obedience* leads to hope and hope leads to obedience. No other group of people have put this principle to the test more than Israel. Sadness, exile and bondage often resulted from Israel's disobedience, but time and time again they were restored to joy in their relationship with God. History was their source for *hope*. When they disobeyed, they never lost hope that God would restore them when they returned to obedience. Obedience brought joy; disobedience led to discipline. Historical hope was consistent; historical hope *is* consistent. Romans 15:4 reminds us that, "Everything that was written in the past was written to teach us. The Scriptures give us patience and encouragement so that we can have hope."

The importance of sharing hope:
"In your hearts set apart Christ as Lord. Always be prepared to give an answer to everyone who asks you to give the reason for the hope that you have."I Peter 3:15

Early in Paul's second letter to the Corinthians we read, "God is the Father who is full of mercy and all comfort. He comforts us every time we have trouble, so when others have trouble, we can comfort them with the same comfort God gives us" (2 Cor 1:3-4). Our relationship with the Father empowers, encourages and instructs us to be a reflection to others of His comfort and hope. Paul goes on to say that "you can help us with your prayers" (1:11). We are to be role models to others of what we have received and we are to impart hope through our prayers.

Scriptural Insights:

The focus of these scriptural references is to give you a biblical understanding of the "Bridge of Hope". (Scriptures are printed in the back of the book.)

1. *Ps 119:81, 114, 116; Ro 5:1-2; Ro 8:23; Tit 2:11-13; Tit 3:4-7; I Pe 1:13; 1 Jn 3:2-3*
What did the writers of Scripture place their hope in, according to these verses?

2. *Ps 43:5; Ps 62:5-6; Ps 130:7; Ps 146:5-6; Hab 3:17-19; 1 Ti 4:10*
Who are we to put our hope in?

3. *Ps 16: 8-11; Ps 25:3, 21; Ps 33:18-22; Ps 119:116 Ps 146: 5-9; Isa 30:18; Isa 40:31; Jer 17:7-8; Lam 3:21-22; Mic 7:7-8; Ro 5:5; Ro 15:13; Eph 1:18; 1 Pe 1:3;*
What are some benefits to those who place their hope in God?

4. *Heb 11:1*
What is the relationship between hope and faith?

5. *1 Pe 3:15; 1 Jn 3:2-3*
Because we have hope, what ought we to do?

Focused Application:

"Despair says circumstances tell us what is true about God. *Hope* says God tells us what is true about circumstances." [9]

I. What is the difference between hoping in the Lord and other kinds of human hope?

II. What tends to rob you of hope (e.g. illness, relationships, financial struggles, current events in your home, community or the world, etc.)?

III. Describe the hope your salvation brings to you.

What else has God done in your life that comforts you and brings you hope?

How might your hope be a bridge to a nonbeliever?

IV. Psalms 120-134 are referred to as the Psalms of Ascent. These 15 psalms were a way for the Hebrew pilgrims to express God's amazing grace and to quiet their fears as they made their pilgrimage to Jerusalem three times each year for the Feast of Passover in the spring, the Feast of Pentecost in early summer and the Feast of Tabernacles in the autumn. Of these 15 psalms, Psalm 130 is referred to as the "Psalm of Hope".

- Verse 5 says, "I wait, and my soul waits." What is the relationship between waiting and hope?

- What does the image of a watchman convey about hope?

- Why are we to hope in the Lord? (vv 7-8)

V. What area(s) of life is it difficult for you to be hopeful about? To what extent is your lack of hope related to a weak connection with God?

To what extent is it related to a need for stronger relationship with other Christians?

VI. I feel most hopeful when . . . . .

CHAPTER 9

The Bridge of Hospitality

Key Scripture: Offer hospitality to one another without grumbling. Each one should use whatever gift he has received to serve others, faithfully administering God's grace in its various forms. I Peter 4: 9-10

Overview:
We all hunger for meaningful relationships. If we were vulnerable, we would even admit to hungering for a warm fire, a pie in the oven, and engaging conversation around the table. Our image of *home* conjures up pictures of acceptance—a place where we feel welcomed and loved. Ultimately, the 'home' with fire burning, pie cooking, and loving acceptance is not realized until we reach Heaven. Our soul longings can only be fully actualized in Christ. Through the extension of relaxed hospitality we can build bridges to those who need Jesus to fulfill their deepest needs.

The "Bridge of Hospitality" study guide addresses the following:

- What it means to be hospitable
- Biblical examples of hospitality
- Providing hospitality to others practically and relationally

Scriptural references throughout provide biblical support for the bridge.

The "Focused Application" segment allows you to apply the scriptural principles addressed in "Core Concepts" and "Scriptural Insights".

Core Concepts:

My Kitchen Prayer

Lord of all pots and pans and things,
since I've not time to be
A saint by doing lovely things
or watching late with Thee
Or dreaming in the dawn light
or storming Heaven's gates,
Make me a saint by getting meals
and washing up the plates.

Although I must have Martha's hands,
I have a Mary mind,
And when I black the boots and shoes,
Thy sandals, Lord, I find.
I think of how they trod the earth,
each time I scrub the floor;
Accept this meditation, Lord,
I haven't time for more.

Warm all the kitchen with Thy love,
and light it with Thy peace;
Forgive me all my worrying
and make my grumbling cease.
Thou who didst love to give men food,
in room or by the sea,
Accept this service that I do,
I do it unto Thee. [1]

What it means to be hospitable:

The dictionary describes hospitality as " the quality or disposition of receiving and treating guests and strangers in a warm, friendly, generous way". Growing up in the Southern culture, I learned at an early age, from the women in my life, how to be hospitable. "Company's comin'!" meant organizing, writing elaborate lists, sweeping the front doorstep, and anticipating the fun ahead. As I have grown in my Christian walk, I have come to view hospitality as Karen Burton Mains explains it. "Hospitality is more than just a human talent, it is a gift of the Holy Spirit. It is a supernatural ministry which, when combined with righteous living, bathed in prayer, and dedicated to the Lord, can be used by God far beyond anything we ask or think". [2] This is not entertaining. Entertaining focuses on us, our abilities, our resources, our convenience. Hospitality's focus is on serving others. "You are sharing a part of yourself. You are opening your home at a time when many people view their homes as retreats in which to hide. This sharing of private space has a way of breaking down relational barriers quickly and naturally. It communicates a genuine interest in people at a time when many people have no local family and are hungry for meaningful relationships".[3] In the dictionary, the word hospitable is found between the words hospice and hospital. A hospice is lodging for travelers or the needy; a hospital is an institution where the sick or injured receive care. That is what it means to be hospitable. We are to open our homes as a place of shelter for the needy and a place of care for the sickly.

Biblical examples of hospitality:

Elizabeth George, in her best-selling book *A Woman's High Calling*, states that historically the Christian home has been used to minister not only to family but to strangers who needed a hotel, a hearth, a haven, a hospital. [4] We should consider it a privilege to follow the examples of women in the Bible who exhibit hospitality:

- 1 Kings 17 – the widow of Zarepheth

- 2 Kings 4 – the Shunammite woman

- Acts 12: 12-17 – Mary

- Acts 16: 13-15, 40 – Lydia

- 1 Corinthians 16:19 – Priscilla

- 1 Timothy 5:10 – the widows

Jesus himself understood the value of spending time over the table at a meal. Remember His meals with Pharisees (Luke 7:36-50, 14: 1-24) and tax collectors (Mark 2:16, Luke 5:27-29)? As to whom we extend our invitations, Jesus reminds us in Luke 14: 12-14 to remember that inviting only our friends and relatives cannot be classified as a spiritual act of true charity. It could also be a rebuke against those prone to reserve their hospitality for rich 'neighbors' whom they know will feel obligated to return the favor.

Providing hospitality to others practically and relationally:

People all around us are longing for closer relationships. How can we extend a welcoming arm to them in this fast-paced society? First of all, it requires a desire to open up your home and yourself to others, unselfishly sharing of your time and energy in order to build relationship. This involves making a list of people to invite and then following through, not just letting it be a good intention. Schedule times on your calendar and contact the people with your available dates. As to who might be included on your list, begin with your neighbors. Are there any new families who have recently moved into the neighborhood? What about single parents or aging couples whose families live out of town? As you branch out, think of coworkers, students at a nearby college, international students, church members, visiting clergy or missionaries, anyone you desire to get to know better or who currently need some encouragement.

For granted, preparation is required, but remember, perfection is not necessary. A little dust helps people relate! The motto of my household is "to be clean enough to be healthy, and dirty enough to be comfortable"! Pray about your guest list, asking God to let you design your event to best bless the people you are having over. Meals can be elaborate or simple. Allow guests to bring a little addition to the meal. That oftentimes makes them feel better about accepting the invitation. During the event allow ample time for each person to talk. Ask sincere questions, share some laughs, and actively listen to one another. Introduce old friends to new people. In short, express Christ's love in practical ways. This will whet a person's appetite and plant a seed that may mature in time to a relationship with each other and Christ. A final reminder is to be comfortable with who you are. This will cause other people to be comfortable as well. People enjoy being around those who express a genuine care for them. In our fast- paced, transient society, making time to build bridges through loving hospitality may be the key to spiritually impacting others for Christ. Through the feeding of the physical body, the spiritual hunger within may obtain nourishment. Ken Gire expresses this so well in *Windows of the Soul.* [5]

A Prayer for Nourishment
How inarticulate are the longings of my soul, O God,
yet how acute are its pangs.
How incapable am I in understanding those longings,
let alone, in tending them.
Feed me with food, O God, that will best nourish my soul,
food that will intensify rather than satisfy
my love for you
and my longing to be with You.
Awaken every eternal seed You have planted in my soul
so while I am yet rooted in this earth
something of heaven might blossom in my life…

Scriptural Insights (Scriptures are printed in the back of the book.)

The focus of these scriptural references is to give you a biblical understanding of the "Bridge of Hospitality".

1. *1 Pe 4:9; Dt. 15:11; Mt. 10:42; 1 Pe 4:11*
God offers several biblical guidelines for hospitality. Identify each one in these scriptures.

2. *Heb. 13:2; Isa. 58:7; Lk 14:13; 2 Ki 6:22-23; Ro. 12:20*
To whom specifically should hospitality be shown?

3. *1 Jn 3:17; Ac 20:35*
What do these verses say about giving of yourself and your resources?

4. *1 Ki 17: 10-16*
2 Ki 4: 8-11
Ac 12: 11-17
Ac 16: 13-15, 40
1 Co 16:19
In the "Core Concepts" several women of the Bible are identified who extend hospitality. Write a description of each one's hospitable action.

5. *Mt 25: 35-36, 40*
How does this verse compare the needy among us to Christ?

6. *Lev 23:22; Isa 58: 6-9; Lk 14: 12-14*
In each of these texts we are commended to hospitality. Record how we are to respond in each instance.

7. *Ac 5: 42*
The church has a mission to be a center for Christian fellowship. How is the church to extend hospitality?

8. *Mt 10: 9-11*
Christ taught that we are to expect hospitality for Kingdom work. Describe how this is to occur.

Focused Application

I. We all need real-life role models for growth in our lives. Answer the following questions to discover your hospitality role models.

- Whom do I know who displays a hospitable nature?
- What do they do to exemplify hospitality to others?
- Why are their examples of hospitality important to me?

II. List all the possible excuses that you might give as reasons for not practicing hospitality. Make a resolve to discipline yourself in some way to change in these areas.

III. Rate your servanthood quotient. In each of the following areas mark yourself in your attitude toward serving others.

USE OF YOUR TIME

Poor————————————Excellent

USE OF YOUR MONEY

Poor————————————Excellent

USE OF YOUR HOME

Poor————————————Excellent

USE OF YOUR POSSESSIONS

Poor————————————Excellent

Decide to make some changes in the areas where you rated poorly.

The Bridge of Hospitality

IV. Hospitality is not just something we extend to guests and strangers. It also applies to those with whom we share our day-to-day existence. Answer the following questions in light of your hospitality toward the people within your family.

- Am I glad to see them at the end of a day apart? What is the tone of my greeting?
- What could I do to bring freshness to a stale relationship?
- Am I not welcoming due to self-centeredness? Resentment?
- Am I affirming and encouraging the development of each person in the family?

V. Practice extending hospitality to the world around you. To get started, contact area college students who could help you identify international students with whom to connect. Consider asking your church secretary to put your family down as a possible host home when traveling missionaries need lodging.

VI. You may have yourself convinced that you do not have the gift of hospitality. Look at the following list of roadblocks and check the ones that apply. Plan to take the checked areas to the Lord and ask Him to help you change into a more hospitable person.

_____Fear of failure. Afraid to take the risk in order to avoid the pain or shame of failing.

_____Resource myopia. Failure to see your strengths. Lack of appreciation for resources you possess.

_____Need for order. Inability to tolerate disorder. Dislike of complexity.

_____Frustration avoidance. Avoiding discomfort at all costs.

_____Self-centeredness. Thinking of less important priorities. Expending energies elsewhere.

CHAPTER 10

The Bridge of Impartiality

Key Scripture: My brothers, as believers in our glorious Lord Jesus Christ, don't show favoritism. James 2:1

Overview:
Being a follower of Christ and showing partiality is incompatible. Judging others solely on external face values, such as education, clothing, cars or color is inconsistent with the teachings of Jesus. It is important to be discerning in regards to other people's character, but not their external characteristics. The writer of James' epistle is dealing with our tendency to be prejudiced toward others because of superficial judgments based on outward appearances. Many relational bridges are never constructed, or may be severely damaged, because of impartiality.

"The Bridge of Impartiality" study guide addresses the following:

- The dangers of bias
- The benefits of impartiality
- Biblical examples of impartiality

Scriptural references throughout provide biblical support for the bridge.

The "Focused Application" segment allows you to apply the scriptural principles addressed in "Core Concepts" and "Scriptural Insights".

Core Concepts:

Webster's defines prejudice as "injury or damage resulting from some judgment or action of another in disregard of one's rights; *esp:* detriment to one's legal rights or claims ... an irrational attitude of hostility directed against an individual, a group, a race, or their supposed characteristics." In its root form, it simply means to prejudge, to form an opinion prematurely on the basis of preconceived ideas. In a sermon delivered by Charles R. Swindoll he states, "Prejudice is powerful. It's tragic, it's cruel, and it knows no bounds. The religious leaders of Jesus' day proved that. So did the educated Nazis who tended their gardens while butchering eleven million men, women, and children. So did Stalin, whose political juggernaut put thirty million to death. Such overwhelming, faceless numbers make it easy to become numb to the real horror of prejudice. And it's easy, too, to think that we would never do such evil, letting ourselves off the hook. But we all have prejudices." [1]

The dangers of bias:

You may not find the word prejudice specifically listed anywhere in the Bible, but you will see the categories under which it falls: evil thoughts, deeds of wickedness, deceit, slander, pride, and foolishness. It is conceived in the realm of the thought life, is given birth in mean-spirited slander, and then comes to horrible maturity in acts of hatred and cruelty. In the words of Christ, "What comes out of a man, that defiles a man. For from within, out of the heart of men, proceed evil thoughts, adulteries, fornications, murders, thefts, covetousness, wickedness, deceit, lewdness, an evil eye, blasphemy, pride, foolishness. All these evil things come from within and defile a man" (Mark 7: 21-23). All of us are born with a sinful nature. We learn specific biases from those around us, most often from someone older in the family system. According to Galatians 5: 19-21, our biases are the results of our flesh, that part of us that is hostile toward God. However, for the Christian, it is God's will for us not to walk according to the flesh, but to walk in the Spirit. Having a bias keeps us from walking in the light of Christ. Our ability to understand truth is like a window through which light enters our hearts. When this window is dirty with bias, the light is obscured and darkness fills the heart. Our minds then blindly base their judgments on a reality that is only dimly understood or may not understood at all. Another danger of having a bias is that we limit ourselves to old, unhealthy thinking and behaviors. This is especially true in the area of relationships. Biased people have little room for new and innovative ways of bringing different people together. When we live with biases, God is not pleased. We are willfully walking outside the will of God. From God's perspective, the main thing we should be most concerned with is the condition of one's soul, not a person's wealth, color, educational status, or any other outward reality. Moses said, "You shall love your neighbor as yourself" (Leviticus 19:18). What was the law then still is today. If you show partiality, you have become a law-breaker. As one commentator observed, "Anyone who shows favoritism breaks the supreme law of love for his neighbor, the law that comprehends all laws governing one's relationships to one's fellowmen". [2]

Would it not be wonderful if the law of love guided all our relationships? The fact is, however, we all have certain biases that taint our reactions to people. We conclude in our minds, I will love you....if. When we choose to walk outside God's plan for relationship, we can expect tremendous difficulty in our lives. We will experience fear, isolation, bitterness, and rage, to name only a few. God cannot and will not bless our relationships while we hold on to our biases. If your eyes are stained with a bias toward others, consider the powerful truth of the following words by C.S. Lewis.

There are no *ordinary* people. You have never talked to a mere mortal. Nations, cultures, arts, civilization—these are mortal, and their life is to ours as the life of a gnat. But it is immortals whom we joke with, work with, marry, snub, and exploit—immortal horrors or everlasting splendours. Next to the Blessed Sacrament itself, your neighbor is the holiest object presented to your senses. If he is your Christian neighbour he is holy in almost the same way, for in him also Christ the glorifier and the glorified, Glory Himself, is truly hidden.[3]

The benefits of impartiality:

It is easy to love Christ—for all He is, for all He has done. It is not so easy, however, to love other people. Yet this is the Lord's command! That compelling mark of the Christian will be a powerful witness to people everywhere. In his book, *A Legacy of Hatred*, David A. Rausch writes,

Are Christians really different from the rest of society? Some Christians throughout Europe not only opposed the Nazis but also helped and defended the Jewish people. They met the challenge that was suddenly thrust upon them. However, they were relatively few in number—a fact that perplexed Richard Gutteridge as he studied the German evangelical response to Nazi racist propaganda. Gutteridge concluded: "Most tragically of all, what was missing was a spontaneous outburst at any point by ordinary decent Christian folk, who certainly existed in considerable numbers". [4]

We "ordinary decent Christian folk" still exist in considerable numbers. But are we standing up and protesting the prejudices of our day? How do we get beyond this, and as a result, become bridge builders? First, we must be obedient to the truth. This means not looking through the distorted lenses of your own bias. You see, God views your bias as sin. Begin to see other people through Christ's eyes and love them as He loves. This obedience to the truth has a purifying effect on us. It purges us not only of a limited perspective, but also of prejudice, resentment, hurt feelings and grudges. This maturity of love toward others does away with hypocrisy, and we can begin to love sincerely. It does not make us blind to each other's faults; it merely gives us the grace to overlook them.

Biblical examples of impartiality:

Follow the example of Christ. He had a powerful influence on what many perceived as the 'nobodies' of this world. The Samaritan woman was amazed that a Jewish man knew everything about her, yet asked her for a drink of water. It was Jesus' impartiality that built a bridge between Himself and that woman. It radically changed her life! She went back to her village astounded and amazed. Her testimony practically brought the entire village to Christ. That is the power of seeing beyond our differences. In another case, Zacchaeus, a hated tax collector, wanted to see Jesus. The local folk did not allow him to press through the crowd to get a glimpse, so he climbed a tree in order to see Jesus. Jesus singles out this "most wretched man" and says to him, " I want to go to your house—come on down." Jesus did not let Zacchaeus's miserable lifestyle keep Him from loving him. The thief on the cross beside Jesus found this same mercy. People who are free from bias are people who exude mercy. There is an unexplainable joy and peace that permeates from their lives. The primary benefit of impartiality is relationship. Impartial people are bridge builders. They are always seeing the possibilities for developing strong connections with others. Loneliness seldom occurs. There is a contagious enthusiasm in their demeanor. These people have been emancipated by the power of the Holy Spirit through the gospel of Jesus Christ! The body of Christ is all-inclusive. All people of all backgrounds can come together for one purpose: to glorify God. The fear of being different is gone. The love of God will take the place of fear. The weight of hostility, rage, and hateful acts will vanish.

These extreme changes can never take place until we allow God to totally transform us through the power of His Spirit. Only the love of God can set us free to love one another at this level of impartiality. There is no room for self-protecting. Old ways of thinking that are not founded in scripture must go. When we begin to operate within the mind of Christ, we will begin to see everybody as a somebody as Jesus did. Our credibility, our witness to the world, is demonstrated by our love for each other. There is no greater witness to the genuineness of our gospel. Obviously, partiality affects more than just racial barriers. If, because of Christ, blacks and whites could live out the model of reconciliation that has not been obtained by any other force, the world would wonder why. It is time for Christians to demonstrate to an unbelieving world a Christian faith more powerful than any other religion. A world watches to see if we can get beyond our words and live out Jesus.

The Bridge of Impartiality

Scriptural Insights:

The focus of these scriptural references is to give you a biblical understanding of the "Bridge of Impartiality."

1. According to *Lev 19:15*, how are we to handle the poor?

2. *Dt. 1:17*
What does this verse tell us about partiality?

3. *Dt. 10:17; Ro 2:11*
What do these verses say about God?

4. *Pr 28:21*
What does this scripture say about a bribe?

5. *Mt 22:16*
As you carefully read this verse, discover the message of impartiality.

6. *Jas 2:9*
Partiality is a sin. How seriously should we take our biases?

7. According to Jesus, who is our neighbor in *Lk 10: 29-37*?

8. In *Jas 2: 1-12*, we are warned to beware of what?

9. *Mk 7: 21-23*
Prejudice is a _____ problem.

Relationship

Focused Application:

I. How much does your upbringing currently influence the way you relate to people of differing race? Explain.

II. Who do you consider to be your neighbor? Compare to Luke 10.

III. Does prejudice make your blood boil, or are you not really bothered by it unless it affects you directly?

IV. When someone tells a racist joke, do you politely but firmly reject such slander?

V. What is your view of the wealthy? The poor? Does a person's outward appearance affect you in any way?

VI. Are you currently building a bridge with anyone you typically would not associate with? Why or why not?

VII. Rate your expression of mercy towards others not like yourself.

0————————————————————————10

VIII. What are some other biases that you are aware of, other than racial. List them.

IX. Why should we build a bridge with others? Is Jesus your example?

X. Finally, formulate the steps you plan to take the next time you recognize personal prejudice. For example:

When I recognize personal prejudice, I will
1. Tell myself that I lack sound information
2.
3.

CHAPTER 11

The Bridge of Integrity

Key Scripture: When a man's ways are pleasing to the Lord, he makes even his enemies live at peace with him. Proverbs 16:7

Dedication: The "Bridge of Integrity" study guide is dedicated
In memory of Howard Taft Williams,
(10/30/1908-11/25/2000)
a Christian gentleman,
my father and friend
who both in his professional life as an educator of young children
and in his personal life as husband, father, grandfather,
great-grandfather, brother and friend,
modeled integrity.
—Martha W. Homme

Overview:
A modern-day biblical thesaurus might give the letters "WWJD" (What would Jesus Do?) as a synonym for "integrity". Everywhere in Christendom today we see "WWJD" on bracelets, key chains, clothing, and much more. Are these letters a constant reminder of biblical integrity or merely a faddish fashion statement? WWJD is not new. The phrase comes from Charles Sheldon's 1897 novel in which a small-town pastor encourages his congregation to live a year based on that question. Sheldon's novel reflects the writing of

fifteenth-century monk Thomas a Kempis in *The Imitation of Christ.* Imitating Christ has long been the goal of Christians pursuing integrity. Imitation requires careful study of that which one desires to imitate; it is also best attained as a result of being in *relationship* with that which one wishes to imitate.

The "Bridge of Integrity" study guide addresses the following:

- What is biblical integrity
- Benefits and costs of living a life of integrity
- Biblical examples of integrity
- How to become people of integrity
- How integrity impacts relationships

Core Concepts:

There is a difference between doing some particular just or temperate action and being a just or temperate man. Someone who is not a good tennis player may now and then make a good shot. What you mean by a good player is the man whose eye and muscles and nerves have been so trained by making innumerable good shots that they can now be relied on. They have a certain tone or quality which is there even when he is not playing, just as a mathematician's mind has a certain habit and outlook which is there even when he is not doing mathematics. In the same way a man who perseveres in doing just actions gets in the end a certain quality of character. Now it is that quality rather than the particular actions which we mean when we talk of virtue. (*a.k.a. integrity*) Italics added. —C. S. Lewis [1]

What is biblical integrity:

Integrity is an uncompromising adherence to moral and ethical principles. A compelling quality of integrity is wholeness. There is no discrepancy between what a person of integrity appears to be on the outside and what he is on the inside. Integrity, for the Christian, means living by the Scriptures.

Integrity is best defined by how it is fleshed out in a

corrupt world. People of integrity keep their word, even when it hurts, are honest in all their dealings, personal and business, and practice morality in their sexual life, both in mind and body. No, they are not perfect. People of integrity sin and make mistakes, but they admit them; they do not cover them up. And they change their lives for the better.

Integrity is important in minor matters as well as major ones. When we dig an ethical grave, it is not with a ditch digger but with a teaspoon, one small choice at a time. [2]

Let's paint a picture of integrity. It first and foremost assumes right and wrong. It is quiet. It deals with the inside, with motives, with ideals, quiet things like keeping commitments. Integrity tells the truth; expects temptation and braces for it; cultivates endurance; and guards the tongue, channeling its power to encourage others and to glorify God. Integrity follows the path of forgiveness. [3]

"Two conditions test the strength of our integrity—adversity and prosperity." [4] Few things reveal how strong or weak we are as does adversity. As King Solomon discerned, "If you falter in times of trouble, how small is your strength" (Prov. 24:10). Solomon also knew a lot about the test of prosperity. He had plenty of first-hand experience letting his prosperity impact his relationship with God. Scottish essayist Thomas Carlyle wrote: "Adversity is sometimes hard upon a man; but for one man who can stand prosperity, there are a hundred that will stand adversity." [5]

Benefits and costs of living a life of integrity:

Integrity works both outwardly and inwardly. Outward synonyms for integrity include forthrightness, goodness, honesty, incorruptibility, principle-centeredness, righteousness, sincerity, straightforwardness and virtue. These characteristics of integrity benefit others. However, integrity also benefits oneself inwardly. A major reason for personal integrity is its impact on integration and wholeness. Personal integrity provides completeness, simplicity, soundness, stability and unity to one's spirit and soul.

In his famous poem, "The Road Less Traveled", Robert Frost talks about two roads. He took the "one less traveled" and that "made all the difference". We have the choice of walking the road of integrity or the road of wickedness. Each decision we make to live in integrity leads us further down the path of peace and order. Rebellion and disobedience, even in the small things of life, bring confusion, distraction and destruction. So what is "all the difference" of taking the road less traveled? Righteousness guards the man of integrity, but wickedness overthrows the sinner (Proverbs 13:6).

Biblical examples of "integrity"

Numerous giants of the faith throughout the Old Testament illustrate the challenges and the rewards of integrity. We are told in Job 2:3 that the Lord, speaking to Satan, said, "Have you considered my servant Job? There is no one on earth like him; he is blameless and upright, a man who fears God and shuns evil. And he still maintains his integrity." Job had just lost his ten children and his immense wealth but his response was to continue to acknowledge God's sovereignty. When Job lost everything, he kept his spiritual integrity. Surely Job grieved, asked why, questioned and begged for answers. What set Job apart was that throughout his tragedies and trials, he did not turn away from his faith or accuse God of wrongdoing. Job practiced integrity in spite of hardship.

During his years of ministry, the prophet Jeremiah suffered intense persecution. He remained faithful to God's call, however. He showed great compassion for his people, even though they mistreated him. He also maintained strong communication with God and fearlessly confronted the Jews per God's instruction. Integrity's cost was great; its eternal benefits, much greater.

Daniel, although a Jewish captive in Babylon, became a high government official there. His exemplary integrity and quality work earned him many enemies. However, "the administration and the satraps tried to find grounds for charges against Daniel in his conduct of government affairs, but they were unable to do so. They could find no corruption in him" (Dan 6:4). Daniel remained true in his worship of the God of Israel while in Babylon. His integrity brought him not only the king's regard but also God's dramatic favor and protection.

David was not an aspiring king; he was simply a shepherd with integrity. His reputation for integrity was not sustained by never falling short, as we well know, but rather because he continually came before God for accountability.
"Then I acknowledged my sin to you and did not cover up my iniquity" (Ps. 32:5). "Create in me a pure heart, O God, and renew a steadfast spirit within me" (Ps. 51:10).

Christ Jesus himself is the consummate example of integrity in the New Testament:
> Who being in very nature God, (Christ Jesus) did not consider equality with God something to be grasped, but made himself nothing, taking the very nature of a servant, being made in human likeness. And being found in appearance as a man, he humbled himself and became obedient to death—even death on a cross! Therefore God exalted him to the highest place and gave him the name that is above every name. (Philippians 2:6-9)

Christ Jesus, perfect and supreme, was willing to give up his throne, take on the nature of man and pay the ultimate price, death on the cross, for us. The cost was great; the eternal benefits, countless. Christ Jesus's integrity makes us whole.

Finally, let us look at a man who was forever changed by his encounter with Christ Jesus. "So I strive always to keep my conscience clear before God and man" (Acts 24:16). Although his early career was anything but exemplary, the Apostle Paul became a man of integrity. As with other giants of the faith, the cost was high, but the eternal benefits were great. The Jews had accused Paul of being a troublemaker, stirring up riots among the Jews all over the world (24:5) Paul was on trial before Felix, Roman governor of

Judea. Felix was well acquainted with the Way (24:22) and their peaceful lifestyles so he chose to put Paul under guard and postpone the decision regarding his case. Felix, taken by Paul's message, "sent for Paul and listened to him as he spoke about faith in Christ Jesus." All was going well until Felix's immoral lifestyle (he was married to another's wife) was challenged by the integrity of Paul's message of righteousness, self-control and the judgment to come (24:25). A man of integrity had spoken. The response is always our free choice.

Paul's integrity was a constant model to others. "You know how we lived among you for your sake. You became imitators of us and of the Lord; in spite of severe suffering, you welcomed the message with the joy given by the Holy Spirit" (I Thes 1:5-7).

How to become people of "integrity":

"Search me, O God, and know my heart; test me and know my anxious thoughts. See if there is any offensive way in me, and lead me in the way everlasting" (Ps 139:23-24). This well known passage from one of the many great psalms of David is one of the keys to his reputation for integrity. David continually called upon God to scrutinize his heart, mind and behaviors. If we desire to be people of integrity, we too must consistently come before God for evaluation, accountability and correction.

Integrity is not attained on our own. Paul constantly credits the Holy Spirit as the power source not only of the gospel but his own ability to share the gospel, in word and deed, with integrity. (I Thes 1:4)

Jerry White in a *Discipleship Journal* article, "The Power of Integrity,"[2] gives five steps to growing in integrity:

Step 1. Deal with the past. Are there areas and activities in your life that lack integrity? Confess them to God and ask His forgiveness. You may also need to confess to others who have been affected by your lack of integrity. Step 1 allows you to clear your mind and conscience so you are able to think biblically.

Step 2. Commit to discovering what the Scriptures say about integrity. Search the Scriptures for what to do and say when you encounter various situations and circumstances. Have a ready, right response.

Step 3. Examine your daily walk with God. Allow the Holy Spirit to stir your conscience.

Step 4. Seek godly counsel from someone who understands your circumstances and lives by God's values.

Step 5. Obey what you know. Do not ignore, but rather respond, to what God asks you to do through:
- His Word
- The urging of the Holy Spirit
- Your conscience, and
- What you simply know is right.

How integrity impacts relationships:

A life of integrity signifies *commitment*. The Old Testament book of Hosea highlights the parallels between the relationship of the prophet Hosea and his wife Gomer with God's relationship with the nation of Israel. Commitment is woven throughout Hosea's story. God told him to find a wife and told him ahead of time that she would be unfaithful to him. Hosea's integrity directed his commitment. He willingly submitted to the Lord's direction; he grieved over the unfaithfulness of his wife, and his people; he found Gomer, redeemed her, and brought her home, fully reconciled. That takes integrity and commitment. Hosea's commitment was not simply to his wife; it was to God. Hosea's life story is a picture of God's love for his people and His response to His bride, the Church. As we relate to others with integrity, we model the commitment the Lord has promised each of us who are in relationship with Him. As we relate to others with integrity, they can count on us to keep our commitments to them.

Relationship

Integrity also connotes predictability, consistency and trustworthiness. When we relate to others with integrity, they know in advance they can expect we will relate from right not wrong and that we will do so consistently. There will not be any surprises; we are not trying to catch them off their guard. God relates to us with predictable integrity. His promises are absolute. "I will make an everlasting covenant with you" (Isa. 55:3). "Believe in the Lord Jesus and you will be saved" (Acts 16:31). "If we confess our sins, he is faithful and just and will forgive us our sins and purify us from all unrighteousness" (I John 1:9).

Those who are guided by integrity also deepen the experience of *safety* and *loyalty* in their relationships. "And Jonathan made a covenant with David because he loved him as himself" (I Sam. 18:3). Jonathan and David related to each other with integrity. They based their friendship on commitment to God. They let nothing come between them. They drew closer when their friendship was tested during David's turbulent days as Saul sought him out. They encouraged each other's faith and trusted each other with their deepest thoughts and closest confidences. Not only was theirs a true friendship but a friendship that was practiced out of safe, loyal integrity.

Scriptural Insights:

The focus of these scriptural references is to give you a biblical understanding of the Bridge of Integrity. (Scriptures are printed in the back of the book.)

1. *I Ch 29:17; Ps. 25:21; Ps. 41:12; Ps 84:11; Ps 112:4; Pr 2:7-8; Isa 57:2*
According to these passages, what are some of the benefits of practicing integrity?

2. *I Ki 9:4-5*
What did God promise Solomon if he walked in integrity? Who was to be Solomon's role model?

3. *Pr. 10:9; Pr 11:3; Pr 13:6; Lk 16:10*
When we practice integrity, among the benefits we experience are deep inner peace and security. What contrasts do we see in these verses between walking in integrity versus not?

4. *Matt 16:26*
This verse speaks not only of salvation but also of living the walk. What does it teach us about the cost of *lack* of integrity?

Relationship

---

5. *Heb 11:32-39*
Loss of success or money are often the worldly cost of integrity. What does this passage tell us about additional prices that many giants of the faith paid because they lived with integrity?

6. *Gal 5:16*
According to this verse, what is the *key* to living with integrity?

7. *Ps 37:7-9; Matt 6:19-21; Rom 12:3; 1 Tim 6:17-19*
What guidelines for living a life of integrity do we find in these passages?

8. *Tit 2:6-8*
In addition to living with integrity, what does this passage tell us to do? How is integrity a key in relationship building?

The Bridge of Integrity

Focused Application:

It is not guided missiles, but guided morals, that is our great need today. —*God's Little Instruction Book II*

I. Where is your current lifestyle on the *Integrity* scale below? Use an "X" to indicate your "integrity factor" today and an "O" to indicate where you want it to move this month:

0_____10

II. How has your integrity been tested lately? Did the testing strengthen your resolve or lead you to compromise? Explain.

III. How is your "integrity factor" impacting (either positively or negatively) your spouse, your children, your friends, and your co-workers?

IV. What steps do you need to take to increase your "integrity factor"?
What one step will you commit to taking today?

V. Who has been a role model of integrity in your life? What traits define their integrity? When was the last time you thanked them for their example? (Perhaps it is time to write them a note or give them a call.)

CHAPTER 12

The Bridge of Intimacy

Key Scripture: My soul thirsts for God, for the living God. When can I go and meet with God? —Psalm 42:2

Overview:
God desires that we be like Christ. Being like Christ is an intimate relationship, a connecting. Through God's Word, His work, His grace and His spirit, we are empowered to attain this connection, this intimacy. While God is at work in us, molding us into the image of His Son, He also encourages us to allow ourselves to be known to others by building a bridge of intimacy to one another.

The "Bridge of Intimacy" study guide addresses the following:
- Intimacy defined
- Intimacy with God
- Barriers to intimacy

Scriptural references throughout provide biblical support for the bridge.

The "Focused Application" segment allows you to apply the scriptural principles addressed in "Core Concepts" and "Scriptural Insights".

Core concepts:

"We are born helpless. As soon as we are fully conscious we discover loneliness. We need others physically, emotionally, intellectually; we need them if we are to know anything, even ourselves." ——C. S. Lewis

Intimacy is being known to each other, actively and from the deepest most inner parts of our being. Intimacy implies a *connectedness* and connectedness requires relationship. Characteristics of intimacy include familiarity, confidence, confidentiality, friendship, affection, and understanding. The experience of intimacy is deep, detailed, inmost, special and trusted.

Well-known psychologist Erik Erikson described the development of personal identity as growing out of certain crises in psychosocial development.[1] These crises result in progress or regress in personality growth. Erikson's underlying assumption is that the growing person is impelled to become aware of and interact with a widening social community. In the course of these interactions, the child, and later the adult, has a chance to develop a healthy personality one characterized by mastery of the environment, unity of function, and the ability to perceive the world and oneself accurately. Erikson's eight stages of psychosocial development and corresponding typical age of occurrence are:

- Trust vs. Mistrust — Infancy
- Autonomy vs. Shame and Doubt — Early Childhood
- Initiative vs. Guilt — Childhood
- Accomplishment vs. Inferiority — School Age
- Identity vs. Confusion — Adolescence
- *Intimacy* vs. Isolation — Young Adulthood
- Generativity vs. Stagnation — Adulthood
- Integrity vs. Despair — Old Age

The crisis of intimacy vs. isolation arises after identity is established, even if it is not fixed. A typical question describing the intimacy vs. isolation stage is "Can one share by giving some piece of his own identity over to another, so the 'we' supplants 'I' in thinking about the present and future?" Stated additionally, "How is one to be close to other people?" The inability to develop intimate relationships leads to psychological isolation.

Intimacy and *transparency* are close cousins. Transparency involves the sharing of oneself. Intimacy involves the mutual sharing. It is possible to be transparent without being intimate if there is no mutuality.

Two kinds of connectedness are necessary to build intimacy. I must personally be participating in the truth about me. When we talk about intimacy we are talking about building a sense of connectedness between another person and me that involves participation in the truth about myself. The second type of connectedness that is necessary to build intimacy is participation in the truth about the other. The relationship nature of intimacy implies mutual sharing.

Real openness, psychological and spiritual availability, mutuality and dependence on each other for the development of respective strengths, all characterize intimacy. Intimacy includes the experience of a range of emotions. Jesus experienced joy with his disciples and friends, sympathy for the sick and lost, anger at legalists, playfulness with children, grief for the brokenhearted and loneliness and anguish in Gethsemane and on the cross.

Intimacy is a skill, but it is a skill that is rarely taught. Most families do not teach intimacy in general to their children. Society does not reward appropriate intimacy in relationships like it rewards production and performance. Emotional intimacy, especially for men, is not reinforced.

Intimacy is a risk. Intimacy involves exploring your inner world and my inner world. It is a calculated risk: I need this other person to really know me, but will I be accepted if they know what is inside? So, we start slowly with bits and pieces and build up to the risky stuff. If we do not like ourselves, or cannot bear to look at what is inside, intimacy could seem like too great a risk.

Intimacy has four levels. The lowest level is the sharing of facts and information. Level two involves the sharing of ideas with others. By level three we are moving to moderate intimacy, such as agreeing with the other's thoughts or ideas. Finally, when level four intimacy is attained, we are willing to share information about ourselves.

Real intimacy does not happen very easily. You must be comfortable and safe to share core information about deeper things like feelings, dreams, fears, joys. If you do not feel safe, or do not know how to share feelings and emotions, it will be hard to reveal your innermost self to anyone else. Intimacy is often developed in safe community. This might be a small growth group, a mentoring relationship or one-on-one discipleship.

Intimacy with God:
Hidden in the challenges of human psychological development is the agenda for Christian spirituality. Spiritual and psychological maturity involves not so much winning (often the criteria for success in work, play and loving) as learning to prevail and to lose, alternating the ability to receive and to let go.

Coupled with the young adulthood development of psychological intimacy is the development of an intimate relationship with one's Lord. The struggle has a price, however, as illustrated by the story of the struggle between Yaweh and Jacob in the Old Testament (Gen. 32).

What does *intimacy* with God look like? It includes, in the core of our soul, the confidence to actually experience God, to know God, to literally feel and enjoy God in a way that stabilizes the soul. Intimacy with God is reflected in an enjoyment of God rather than a relationship with Him that *uses* Him. Intimacy with God involves personal truth rather than instrumental truth. Instrumental truth is truth that works to serve our purposes. Instrumental truth tends to be based on principles rather than relationships. Personal truth is a relationship. It is discovering what it means to come into the presence of God. It is experiencing one's body as the temple of the Holy Spirit. It is coming to the place of enjoying God supremely so that we will not *demand* intimacy from any other thing or person. When we celebrate this level of intimacy with God, we are free to share intimacy with others.

Intimacy is reflected in the Godhead. God is a community, a trinity of Father, Son and Holy Spirit. 'No man is an island.' Even Jesus's well being depended on intimacy with the Father and the Holy Spirit.

Barriers To Intimacy:
Enmeshed and/or rigid relationships impede appropriate development of intimacy. *Fear* is also a major player in our lack of intimacy. We fear rejection, which is loss of relationship and thus avoid the connectedness that would enhance the relationship. Other barriers to the development of intimacy include:
- Insecurity
- Shame
- Pride
- Busyness
- Avoidance
- Despair and hopelessness based on past experiences, and
- Passivity

The development of intimacy is a high level skill that carries with it numerous risks; however, the benefits of opening oneself both to intimacy with God and with each other are well worth the process of such development.

Scriptural Insights:

The focus of these scriptural references is to give you a biblical understanding of the "Bridge of Intimacy". (Scriptures are printed in the back of the book.)

1. *Ps 139*
This very well known psalm, a favorite of many, talks about the intimate way God knows us. Summarize the psalmist's thoughts.

2. *Jn 15:1-15*
What does this well-known passage tell us about the intimate relationship we have with God through Christ?

3. *Eph 3:16-19*
What do we learn from this passage about knowing God deeply?

4. *Php 2:5; Php 4:8; 2 Co 10:5*
What instructions do these verses provide regarding intimacy of thought?

Relationship

Focused Application:

I. Briefly summarize your faith journey:

What experiences have contributed to the development of your relationship with God?

What bridges have you crossed?

Describe the *intimacy* you are experiencing with God?

II. Below is a list of 10 areas of intimacy.

With whom do you share each of these areas of intimacy? How satisfied are you with your experience of each area?

1. Emotional Intimacy: The sharing of one's self through self-disclosure and inviting self-disclosure of other(s) i.e., the opening of one's deepest feelings to another person.

2. Intellectual Intimacy: The sharing of any thoughts or experiences that stimulated a person such as something read, heard, or observed.

3. Spiritual Intimacy: Simply stated, an individual's shared daily relationship with God (Father, Son and Holy Spirit).

4. Recreational Intimacy: Sharing an activity requiring some form of recreational exertion, such as bicycling, jogging, or playing tennis.

5. Social Intimacy: The sharing that comes in any social setting, ranging from a dinner party to attending movies or athletic events.

6. Household Intimacy: The sharing developed in the course of regular household chores or special home projects. This includes everything from grocery shopping to building an extra room.

7. Vocational Intimacy: Approximately 40 hours of our week are spent at a job. This produces a great deal to share with others.

Intimacy areas 8 through 10 are reserved for marriage. If you are married, how satisfied are you with your experience of each of these areas of intimacy?

8. Genital Intimacy: Because the term "sex" has such wide connotations, "genital" specifies intimacy related to genital foreplay, intercourse, touching, etc.

9. Economic Intimacy: All areas related to finances such as budgeting, property management, investments, speculations, etc.

10. Parenting Intimacy: Any activity relating to children.

III. How would you distinguish between *intimacy* and *transparency*? Are you more intimate or transparent with others? Explain.

CHAPTER 13

The Bridge of Love

Key Scripture: "And he has given us this command: Whoever loves God must also love his brother. 1 John 4:21

Overview:
To love is the highest form of spiritual and emotional maturity. Larry Crabb states, "The more I reflect on the love that Paul spoke of in I Corinthians 13, the more I am persuaded that few people love. Nice people are not hard to find. Churches, neighborhood parties, and civic clubs are full of friendly people."[1]

To love means to come toward another person without self-protection. To love and serve someone, because you have their highest good in mind is risky. If the object of our love chooses to reject or neglect us, the pain becomes unbearable. Our example of love, Christ, kept on loving despite how He was treated. We will continue to love if we are growing into His likeness.

The "Bridge of Love" study guide addresses the following:
- Christ's example of loving
- Choices that bring us to a mature love

Scriptural references throughout provide Biblical support for the bridge.

The "Focused Application" segment allows you to apply the scriptural principles addressed in "Core Concepts" and "Scriptural Insights".

Core Concepts:

Christ's Example of Loving:

To love means to esteem others greater than ourselves. Jesus Christ, as always, is the supreme example. "He made himself nothing, taking the very nature of a servant, being made in human likeness And being found in appearance as a man, he humbled himself and became obedient to death, even death on a cross" (Ph. 2:7-8). Jesus Christ chose to humble himself and give up his kingly rights in order to love.

Self-giving love is more concerned with giving than receiving. Love is action, not abstraction. Love is patient with people and gracious to them with generosity. "Love is patient, love is kind. It does not envy, it does not boast, it is not proud. It is not rude, it is not self-seeking, it is not easily angered, it keeps no record of wrongs. Love does not delight in evil but rejoices with the truth. It always protects, always trusts, always hopes, always perseveres. Love never fails" (1 Co 13:4-8a).

Jesus Christ embodied all of these characteristics of love, because He is love. Jesus never avoided the unloving person. He did not allow fear or anger to keep him from others. Luke 19:10 points out that he came to seek and to save those who were lost. Jesus prayed for His enemies. This shows the great extent of His love. While on the cross He prayed, "Father, forgive them, for they do not know what they are doing" (Lk 23:34). These people did not recognize Him as the true Messiah. They were blind to the light of divine truth. Still their ignorance certainly did not mean that they deserved His love and forgiveness; rather, their spiritual blindness itself was a manifestation of their guilt. Christ's prayer while they were in the very act of mocking Him is an expression of the boundless love of God.

The submissive obedience Christ displays on the cross is the greatest form of love. Though sinless, He took upon Himself the sins of the entire world. He went through false accusations, being beaten beyond recognition, nailed to a cross, dying in agony, alone, for you and me. "Greater love has no one than this, that he lay down his life for his friends." (Jn 15:13). This is a reference to the supreme evidence of Jesus' love. Christians are called to exemplify the same kind of sacrificial giving toward each other, even if such sacrifice involves the laying down of one's own life in imitation of Christ's example.

Christ showed love through the relationships He had with others. From His first miracle at the wedding feast, to His encounter with Peter after the resurrection, Jesus repeatedly showed love toward others. In John 4 Jesus takes time out with a Samaritan woman. While her life-style was ungodly, Jesus relates to her. From this encounter the woman is set free from her sinful life-style and tells the entire village about what Jesus has done for her. He simply built a relationship with her, through loving her, despite her self-centered behavior. His love transformed her life.

In the gospels we see Jesus healing numbers of people because of His great compassion. He told the story about the Good Samaritan helping the victim who had been beaten and robbed. Jesus emphasized in this story the power of compassion. He defined compassion as love in action.

Jesus loved a woman caught in adultery in John, chapter 8. The scribes and Pharisees brought this woman to Him. These religious men were ready to stone her, but Jesus said "If any one of you is without sin, let him be the first to throw a stone at her" (Jn 8:7). The religious men walked away and Jesus was left alone with this woman. Jesus said to her, "Then neither do I condemn you. Go now and leave your life of sin" (Jn 8:11). The impartiality of Christ's love is a great comfort to all of us.

Yet another story emerges from off the pages of scripture. "Jesus loved Martha and her sister and Lazarus" (Jn 11:5). Lazarus died and Jesus came to comfort Mary and Martha. The story includes the fact that Jesus wept over the grief of Lazarus' sister and the loss of a friend. Jesus' love counsels Martha and reassures her that He is "the resurrection and the life" (Jn 11:25). The intimacy of His relationship with Mary, Martha and Lazarus is noteworthy.

Jesus' unconditional love repeatedly springs from the pages of God's Word. With this great truth in mind, Jesus leaves us with a commandment, as His followers: "A new commandment I give you: Love one another. As I have loved you, so you must love one another. By this all men will know that you are my disciples, if you love one another" (Jn 13: 34-35).

Choices That Bring Us to a Mature Love:

It should be clear from what we have discussed thus far that Christ-like love cannot be obtained apart from a growing personal relationship with Jesus Christ. Only through Him do we receive the Holy Spirit and the fruit of His power: ""love, joy, peace, patience, kindness, goodness, faithfulness, gentleness and self-control" (Gal 5:22-23a).

Therefore, if we want to personally experience and publicly express authentic love, we must submit ourselves to Christ in faith. Of course we can refuse to embark on this road of obedience—the road of genuine Christian love. After all, the *Christ-living* way demands personal sacrifice and opens us up to potential heartache and abuse. How much easier it would be to keep to ourselves, striving to satisfy only our own needs and wants. Yet, as C.S. Lewis points out, the toll of living a self-centered life can be extremely high: "There is no safe investment. To love at all is to be vulnerable. Love anything, and your heart will certainly be wrung and possibly be broken. If you want to make sure of keeping it intact, you must give your heart to no one, not even to an animal. Wrap it carefully around with hobbies and little luxuries; avoid all entanglements; lock it up safe in the casket or coffin of your selfishness. But in that casket—safe, dark, motionless, airless—it will change. It will not be broken; it will become unbreakable, impenetrable, and irredeemable. The alternative to tragedy, or at least to the risk of tragedy, is damnation. The only place outside of Heaven where you can be perfectly safe from all the dangers and perturbations of love is Hell." [2]

Fallen human nature is committed to minimizing further damage to our fragile souls by avoiding whatever may hurt and by doing whatever brings the relief of immediate pleasure. All of us have been victimized by others. Living in a fallen world means to live as a damaged person. It is the commitment to avoid further damage that interferes with our efforts to love. For most of us, love is not the bottom line; self-protection is. Love combats against these realities.

"In this way, love is made complete among us so that we will have confidence on the day of judgment, because in this world we are like him. There is no fear in love. But perfect love drives out fear, because fear has to do with punishment. The one who fears is not made perfect in love" (1 Jn 4:17-18). According to this scripture, a person with mature love has confidence in the face of judgment.

Confidence is a sign of mature love. If Jesus called God Father, so may we, since we are accepted in the Beloved. The love that builds confidence also banishes fears. We love God and reverence Him, but we do not love God and come to Him in love and at the same time hide from Him in terror. Fear involves torment or punishment, a reality the sons of God will never experience, because they are forgiven.

Choosing to walk in these truths is a daily discipline. To live and to relate with God and others lovingly begins with an act of the will. "For God did not give us a spirit of timidity, but a spirit of power, of love and of self-discipline." (2 Tim 1:7) God has given believers all the spiritual resources they need for every trial and threat. Divine power—effective, productive spiritual energy belongs to believers. As children of God we have been given love. This love will center on pleasing God and seeking others' welfare before one's own. Lastly, according to 2 Timothy 1:7, we have been given a sound mind. This refers to a disciplined, self-controlled, and properly prioritized mind. A sound mind is the opposite of fear and cowardice that causes disorder and confusion. God's spirit empowers believers to live their lives in Godly wisdom and confidence. Loving God and loving others will be the result of walking in these truths. Every follower of Christ must choose throughout the day, in every situation, "Am I going to walk in the truth or is fear going to control my thoughts and behavior?" We must make that choice.

Larry Crabb writes, "Something is different about people who love. They convey a presence that goes beyond the words they say and the things they do. We know they are for us. In their presence, our growth seems more appealing to us than required of us. Because the relationship is never at stake, we sense a freedom to enter fully into the enjoyment of relationship rather than keep the relationship intact." [3]

Building the *bridge of love* requires choosing the road of selflessness, rather than the road of selfishness. It is through this all-important decision that God enables us to love as He first loved us.

The Bridge of Love

Scriptural Insights:

The focus of these scriptural references is to give you a biblical understanding of the "Bridge of Love". (Scriptures are printed in the back of the book.)

1. The scriptures below illustrate Jesus' love. What do you learn about Him in each of the passages? (Note parallel references are given when appropriate.)

a. *Ps 91:14; Jn 14:31*

b. *Jn 15:9; Eph 5:24*

c. *Pr 8:17; Jn 14:21*

d. *Lk 19:10*

e. *Lk 23:34*

f. *Gal 2:20*

g. *Jn 15:13; 1 Jn 3:16*

h. *Rev 1:5*

i. *Heb 7:25; 9:24*

j. *Ps 68:18; Jn 16:7*

k. *Rev 3:19*

l. *Song of Sol 8:7*

m. *2 Co 5:14*

n. *Jn 13:1*

o. *Ro 8:35*

2. The scriptures below illustrate the love we are to have for one another. What do you discover as you research these scriptures?

a. *1 Jn 4:7*

b. *1 Jn 4:21*

c. *Jn 13:34; 15:12; 1 Jn 3:23; Eph 5:2*

d. *Ga 5:22; Col 1:8*

e. *1 Pe 1:22*

f. *1 Co 13:4-7*

g. *1 Th 1:3; Heb 6:10*

h. *1 Co 13:8,13*

i. *Mt 22:37-39*

j. *1 Co 13:1-2*

k. *Php 1:9; 1 Th 3:12*

l. *Ro 12:9; 2 Co 6:6; 8:8; 1 Jn 3:18*

m. *1 Pe 1:22*

n. *Ga 6:10*

o. *Mt ch. 25*

p. *Eph 4:32*

Focused Application:

I. According to 1 Corinthians, chapter 13, is love optional or essential?

II. Is Christ-like love an essential ingredient in your life? Explain. If not, why not?

III. Do you place a high premium on the development of love in your relationships?

IV. Would your family, your work associates, and others who are close to you agree that your life is characterized by authentic love? Why or why not?

V. Is your love only internal?

VI. Do you let people know through your words and deeds that you care for them? (Love is a magnet that draws us together.)

VII. How would you rate yourself on each of the following statements:

      never   seldom   often   always

    _____ I accept people as they are.

    _____ I believe people are valuable.

    _____ I care when others hurt.

    _____ I desire only what is best for others.

    _____ I erase all offenses.

VIII. Are people drawn to you?

IX. Do they find you to be accepting, caring, patient, and forgiving?

X. Do you give of yourself without expecting anything in return, or do you help others for human recognition and earthly reward? (Love is a long-term investment, not a quick-return loan.)

XI. Does your love have staying power? Explain.

XII. When people treat you unfairly or let you down, how do you respond?

XIII. Are you really committed to reaching out to others, regardless of the personal cost or lack of public applause?

XIV. Do you try to love others as Christ loves you—unselfishly, unconditionally, and abundantly?

XV. Do you currently have an accountability partner who confronts you about your self-protection and/or encourages you when you love others the way Christ would?

CHAPTER 14

The Bridge of Prayer

Key scripture: Therefore, confess your sins to each other and pray for each other so that you may be healed. The prayer of a righteous man is powerful and effective. James 5:16

Overview:
Prayer is a relationship. When Jesus taught His disciples to pray, He began His prayer with "Our Father". The first two words of this model prayer (Matthew 6:9-13) suggest relationship. "Our" reminds us of the importance of praying with and for others. "Father" indicates an intimate, trusting, personal and loving relationship with God, our Heavenly Father. Matthew 18:20 reminds of the relational characteristic of prayer: "For where two or three come together in my name, there am I with them." Our individual prayers bring us into relationship with God; our corporate prayers bring us into relationship with both God and each other. When we intercede for one another in prayer, the relational bridge is strengthened.

The "Bridge of Prayer" study guide addresses the following:

- What is prayer
- Why pray
- Prayer principles
- Prayer as active, radical participation

- Models for prayer
- Challenges and difficulties of prayer
- Praying when life gets difficult
- Praying in Jesus' name

Core Concepts:

O Lord, here I am again. Just plain old me coming to You as I've come a thousand times—And this is what always happens. Your response is immediate. You open Your arms unhesitatingly. You draw me to Yourself. You clasp me to Your Father-heart. Then You reaffirm my position: I am a child of the King and all that is Yours is mine. When I begin my stammering account of gross unworthiness, Your gentle smile hushes me. With endless patience You remind me once more that my value never determines Your love. Rather, Your love determines my value. —Ruth Harms Calkin [1]

Unlike Ruth Harms Calkin, "Most of us are plagued with a subtle aversion to praying. We do not naturally delight in drawing near to God. We pay lip service to the delight and potency and value of prayer. We assert that it is an indispensable adjunct of mature spiritual life. We know that it is constantly enjoined and exemplified in the Scriptures. But in spite of all, too often we fail to pray." [2]

What is prayer:

The desire of God's heart is to be in communication with us. He wants to speak; He wants to listen. God speaks both through His Word and through prayer. He also listens through prayer. Prayer is also the privilege we have to speak to and listen to God. Prayer is our "direct line" relationship with God. [3]

Why pray:

In his comprehensive, compelling primer on prayer, Richard Foster classifies prayer into 3 movements coinciding with the trinity: [4]
- the movement inward, prayer to God the Son, Jesus Christ, corresponding to His role as Savior and Teacher
- the movement upward, prayer to God the Father, corre-

sponding to His role as sovereign King and eternal Lover and
- the movement outward, prayer to the Holy Spirit, corresponding to His role as Empowerer and Evangelist.

Prayer moving us inward allows us to seek the transformation we need; moving upward, we seek needed intimacy; moving outward provides for needed ministry.

God calls us to prayer. Answered prayer begins with Him. Prayer is God's way of accessing us to His divine mind. Biblical men and women of prayer illustrate praying for wisdom regarding what God wanted. They also offered God reasons to grant their requests. Four reasons God answers prayer are:
- the prayer acknowledges God
- the prayer is supported by the intercession of Jesus
- the prayer is supported by the intercession of the Holy Spirit
- the prayer comes from one who is related to God and Christ [5]

Prayer Principles:

God invites us to pray. He also provides prayer principles to guide our prayer relationship with Him:[6]

- *Ask in the Spirit:* All our prayers ought proceed from the mind of the Spirit, not from selfish motives or self-serving ends.
- *Ask with the mind*: Form your requests precisely and specifically from a focused mind.
- *Ask in Jesus' name*: "You may ask me for anything in my name and I will do it" (John 14:14). Asking in Jesus' name requires that we act like him, having His qualities, desires, attitude and outlook. This requires that we first ask before praying, "What would Jesus want in this situation?"
- *Ask while abiding in Christ*: "If you remain in me and my words remain in you, you shall ask whatever you wish, and it will be given you" (John 15:7) Prayer is both a means of abiding in

Relationship

Christ and a result of abiding in Christ.
- *Ask in faith:* God cares about us. We are to make our requests without doubting. We are to believe that when we ask according to His principles, He will answer.
- *Ask in humility:* Praying in humility means we understand our need for God; when we understand our need for God, we are most able to pray with humility.
- *Ask in sincerity:* Genuine, heartfelt prayers result from a serious, earnest, fervent, sincere attitude toward prayer.
- *Ask with perseverance:* "Ask and it will be given to you; seek and you will find; knock and the door will be opened to you. For everyone who asks receives; he who seeks finds; and to him who knocks, the door will be opened" (Matthew 7:7). God wants us to pray persistently to take our eyes off circumstances and put them on Him.

Prayer as active, radical participation:

Scripture instructs us to "ask, seek and knock" (Matthew 7:7). To ask, seek and knock requires that we be actively involved. Christ warns against meaningless repetition in prayer (Matthew 6:7). Prayer is not to be mechanical and impersonal but rather persistent and specific. New Testament Christians were exhorted to devote themselves to prayer and to stay alert. They were to pray continually, giving thanks in all circumstances. Prayer was to be their substitute for any form of anxiety. Praying radically leads to personal and relational growth. When we pray radically, we ask God to stretch us, search us, break us and lead us. [3]

Models for prayer:

Nehemiah 9, the longest recorded prayer in the Bible is a model for four-dimensional praying.[7] In verses 5-6, the prayer *looks up* in adoration and praise. In verses 7-31, it *looks back:* in reflection and thanksgiving. In verses 32-37, the Israelites *look around.* in petition and confession. Finally, in verse 38, the prayer *looks ahead* in direction and commitment. These four dimensions of Israel's prayer serve as a guide for us:

- Praising—looking up
- Reflecting—looking back
- Petitioning—looking at the situation
- Commitment—looking ahead

Brenda Poinsett[8] describes Jesus's four patterns of prayer
- withdrawal
- thanksgiving
- honesty
- intercession

Jesus regularly *withdrew* from continual interruptions from people to commune with God in solitude. These times of prayer were not snippets, but lengthy blocks of time allowing Him to think, express Himself and to listen and wait for His Father's responses. *Thanksgiving* was a noticeable part of Jesus's prayer life. He thanked God before His Father even gave answers to His prayers and He trusted in God's ways. During both difficult times and times of joy, Jesus prayed "even so, Father; for so it seemed good in thy sight". Jesus' *honesty* in prayer is best illustrated in His prayer in Gethsemane (Mt. 26:39). When Jesus prayed for a way out, God gave Him the courage He needed to face the cross. Jesus' intercession is recorded throughout the gospels and continued through His hanging on the cross. (Brenda Poinsett's newest book is *Reaching Heaven: Discovering the Cornerstones of Jesus' Prayer Life*, published by Moody Press, 2002.)

Models for prayer are found in both the Old and New Testaments. Two of the best known models for prayer are the Lord's Prayer (Matthew 6:9-13 and Luke 11:2-4) and the popular ACTS format (adoration, confession, thanksgiving and supplication). In contrast to the lengthy prayer in Nehemiah 9, the Lord's Prayer is brief but comprehensive. Adoration, confession, and supplication are included with thanksgiving implied. A.C.T.S. reminds us of the priority focus of our prayer. We are to worship first and ask later. Furthermore, authentic prayer is identified as that which is done secretly, sincerely and specifically. Prayer is a love relationship and is to be both engaged in intimately and in intimate settings.

Challenges and difficulties of prayer

Among the greatest challenges of prayer is the remembrance that prayer involves both speaking and listening. We are to *wait* upon the Lord, which is no easy assignment in our instant gratification society.

A second challenge is our willingness to admit that God answers all of our prayers. He may not, however, answer them as we asked. When our request to God is wrong, He says, "No". When we are wrong, God says, "Grow". Finally, when our timing is wrong, God says, "slow". [3]

Praying when life gets difficult:

Among the suggestions Nancy Nordenson[9] gives for praying when life gets hard are:
- Find a prayerful place. (Go to a solitary place, just as Jesus did.)
- Use others' words. (Pray the scriptures and/or meaningful prayers prepared by others.)
- Meditate on Jesus' life.
- Pray a repeated phrase. (The benefit is not in the repetition, but rather in the power of repeated phrases to focus our thoughts.)
- Remember the Holy Spirit's intercession. (We do not have to go it on our own.)
- Assume a prayer posture.
- Write the prayer down.
- Pray with our tears.
- Express our anger.
- Be silent.
- Ask others to pray.

Praying in Jesus' name:

Lastly, how often do we end our prayers in Jesus' name? What does it mean to pray in Jesus' name? When we pray in Jesus' name, "we affirm three great realities made possible by His sacrifice for us" [10]

- Authority: Praying in Jesus's name acknowledges the authority of His sacrificial life and death. This authority allows us to come with confidence before God's throne of grace (Hebrews 4:16). Jesus' name also gives us authority over Satan and his angels (Luke 10:17).

- Acceptance: When we pray in Jesus' name, we are reminded of why our relationship with God is even possible. Only through knowing God's Son, Jesus Christ, are we able to come boldly before God.

- Abiding: Finally, when we pray in Jesus' name, we affirm our ongoing relationship with Him. Jesus promised that whatever we ask the Father in His name will be granted (John 14:13, 15:16). This promise is given in the context of our maintaining an abiding relationship of obedience and friendship with Him (John 15:1-8).

Scriptural Insights:

The focus of these scriptural references is to give you a biblical understanding of the Bridge of Prayer. (Scriptures are printed in the back of the book.)

1. Nehemiah 9 is the longest recorded prayer in the Bible. Verses 1-2 give the context of the prayer: humility and purity.
   - By fasting the Israelites were declaring that their hunger for knowing God was priority over satisfying physical hunger.
   - Sackcloth clothing symbolized mourning, humiliation and grief over their sin.
   - By throwing dirt upon themselves they acknowledged identification with death and feelings of deep despair.

This prayer reaches in four directions:
   - looking up in praise (vv. 5-6)
   - looking back in reflection and thanksgiving (vv. 7-31)
   - looking around in petition (vv. 32-37)
   - looking ahead in commitment (vs. 38)

a. What attributes of God do the Israelites praise?

b. Summarize the Israelites moral and physical wanderings as reflected upon in vv. 7-31.

c. Point out the verses in this section of the prayer that indicate that in spite of their dismal history the Israelites saw God as gracious, merciful and compassionate.

d. What petitions does Israel make in vv. 32-37?

e. What is the significance of vs. 38 in the overall intent of this prayer?

2. *Jer. 29:12; Jer. 33:3; Mt. 26:41; Heb 4:16; Jas 5:13-16*
What do these verses tell us about why we need to pray?

3. *Eph 6:18; I Th 5:17*
When are we to pray?

4. *Dt. 4:7; 2 Ch 7:14; Isa. 30:19; Jas 5:15.*
What benefits do we derive from praying?

5. *Ps 46:10; Mt 6:5-8; Mk 11:25; Col 4:2*
What guidelines do these passages give us about how to pray? How not to pray?

6. *Job 22:27; Isa 65:24; Mt 7:7-8; Mt 21:22; Mk 11:24; Jn 14:13-14; Jn 16: 23-24; I Pe 3:12; I Jn 3:21-22; I Jn 5:14-15.*
Under what conditions will God answer our prayers according to these verses?

7. *Rom 8:26-27*
When we are unable to pray on our own, who intercedes for us?

Focused Application:

Our ordinary views of prayer are not found in the New Testament. We look upon prayer as a means of getting things for ourselves; The Bible idea of prayer is that we may get to know God Himself.
—Oswald Chambers

What is the use of praying if at the very moment of prayer we have so little confidence in God that we are busy planning our own kind of answer to our prayer? —Thomas Merton

The fewer words, the better the prayer. —Martin Luther

God answers sharp and sudden on some prayers, and thrusts the thing we have prayed for in our face, a gauntlet with a gift in it.
—Elizabeth Barrett Browning

Why is it when we talk to God we are said to be praying and when God talks to us we're said to be schizophrenic? —Lily Tomlin

I. "Prayer is an end to isolation. It is living our daily life with someone, with him who alone can deliver us from solitude." —Georges Lefevre as quoted in *The One Year Book of Personal Prayer* [11]

How does prayer bring an end to isolation? To what extent has prayer
brought you out of isolation into relationship?

II. Indicate the extent to which you believe prayer makes a difference?

0_____10

III. When do you readily choose to pray?

IV. What are some of the distractions you experience when you attempt to pray?

V. Under what circumstances are you reluctant to pray?

VI. How likely are you to pray when you feel you are facing an impossible situation? In what ways does prayer make a difference when you are faced with an impossible situation?

VII. In what ways do we pray differently when we pray out of helplessness?

VIII. "Always pray about a matter before you talk to another person about it."
Is this a commitment you feel Christians ought to make? Why? Why not?

IX. Below is an excerpt from Henri Nouwen's journal,[12] written in his last year of life. What are your reactions to this quote on prayer from a well-known spiritual guru?

> Prayer is the bridge between my unconscious and conscious life. Prayer connects my mind with my heart, my will with my passions, my brain with my belly. Prayer is the way to let the life-giving Spirit of God penetrate all the corners of my being. Prayer is the divine instrument of my wholeness, unity, and inner peace.
>
> So, what about my life of prayer? Do I like to pray? Do I want to pray? Do I spend time praying? Frankly, the answer is no to

The Bridge of Prayer

all three questions. After sixty-three years of life and thirty-eight years of priesthood, my prayer seems as dead as a rock. I remember fondly my teenage years, when I could hardly stay away from the church. For hours I would stay on my knees filled with a deep sense of Jesus' presence. I couldn't believe that not everyone wanted to pray. Prayer was so intimate and so satisfying. It was during these prayer-filled years that my vocation to the priesthood was shaped. During the years that followed I have paid much attention to prayer, reading about it, writing about it, visiting monasteries and houses of prayer, and guiding many people on their spiritual journeys. By now I should be full of spiritual fire, consumed by prayer. Many people think I am and speak to me as if prayer is my greatest gift and deepest desire.

The truth is that I do not feel much, if anything, when I pray. There are no warm emotions, bodily sensations, or mental visions. None of my five senses is being touched—no special smells, no special sounds, no special sights, no special tastes, and no special movements. Whereas for a long time the Spirit acted so clearly through my flesh, now I feel nothing. I have lived with the expectation that prayer would become easier as I grow older and closer to death. But the opposite seems to be happening. The words *darkness* and *dryness* seem to best describe my prayer today.

Maybe part of this darkness and dryness is the result of my overactivity. As I grow older I become busier and spend less and less time in prayer.

Are the darkness and dryness of my prayer signs of God's absence or are they signs of a presence deeper and wider than my senses can contain? Is the death of my prayer the end of my intimacy with God or the beginning of a new communion, beyond words, emotions, and bodily sensations?

The year ahead of me must be a year of prayer, even though I say that my prayer is as dead as a rock. My prayer surely is, but not necessarily the Spirit's prayer in me. Maybe the time has come to let go of my prayer, my effort to be close to God, my way of being in communion with the Divine, and to allow the Spirit of God to blow freely in me.

CHAPTER 15

The Bridge of Transparency

Key Scripture: Always be prepared to give an answer to everyone who asks you to give the reason for the hope that you have. But do this with gentleness and respect. I Peter 3:15

Overview:
Why do we struggle with being known, with revealing who we are, what we struggle with, what makes us 'tick', what brings us joy or sorrow? "Transparency is traumatic. Open communication is like getting an immunization shot. It hurts, but it helps. It is traumatic to take down the no trespassing sign and invite others to step in. But at the same time, it is so fulfilling to accept and be accepted, love and be loved."[1] "The purposes of a man's heart are deep waters, but a man of understanding draws them out" (Proverbs 20:5). God wants us to feel safe both in a transparent relationship with Him and with others. Too often we keep our relationships at a distant, shallow level by avoiding the risks of revealing our true self and our true needs to others.

The "Bridge of Transparency" study guide addresses the following:

- What it means to be transparent
- Relating transparently to God and Others: The "How To's" and the "How Not To's" of Transparency

Relationship

Scriptural references throughout provide biblical support for the bridge.

The "Focused Application" segment allows you to apply the scriptural principles addressed in "Core Concepts" and "Scriptural Insights".

Core Concepts:

What it means to be transparent:

"We all long for close relationships. Bonds so secure that we can be completely honest and vulnerable. But often, we keep our relationships at a safe and shallow level. We avoid the risk of revealing all that is in our hearts. God wants us to take that risk. His reward for doing so is the satisfaction of true, deep community."[2]

We were created to be transparent. Transparency was the communication norm in the Garden of Eden prior to the Fall. God, man and woman were involved in completely open and honest communication with one another. They experienced, for a time, that delicately balanced combination of truth and transparency that the world now longs for and struggles to attain.

"I long to see you so that I may impart to you some spiritual gift to make you strong—that is, that you and I may be mutually encouraged by each other's faith." So speaks the Apostle Paul in Romans 1:11-12. Although Paul was their mentor, he longed for the Roman believers to be transparent and share of themselves with him also.

What does it mean to be transparent? The dictionary defines transparent as easily understood; obvious. A second definition, though referring to physics, connotes a mystical characteristic of transparency: transmitting rays of light through its substance so that objects beyond can be distinctly seen. When we as Christians are transparent, the rays of light are Jesus, the light of the world (John 8:12). Synonyms for transparent include: articulate, candid, direct, explicit, forthright, frank, honest, sincere, straightforward, undisguised, visible. Transparent people tend to be substantive, deep and lasting. The bonds between transparent relationships allow complete honesty and vulnerability. We grow in maturity and unity as transparency between us increases.

Transparency Lost: Man's "fall" converted the natural practice of transparency into the tendency to *hide* (Gen 3:7-11) and the tendency to *hurl* (Gen 3: 12-13). We hide from one another in numerous ways. We cover up our needs. We bury our thoughts. We repress our feelings. We mull things over inwardly. We are quiet, reserved, or even withdrawn. We are introverted. Sullen. Pouting. Shy. Bashful. We say, "I couldn't care less," but we really do. We say, "Leave me alone," because we don't want anyone to step inside and see what is really happening. We say, "I don't want to talk about it," even though we desperately need to. We say, "Nothing is bothering me," when in all honesty a problem is clawing our soul to shreds. We say, "I can work this out by myself," when in reality we can not; we need help.

We also *hurl* in various ways. "We act as judge and jury and condemn others. We project our problems on those who live with us. We ridicule. We dominate. We are dogmatic, We are sarcastic, obnoxious, overbearing. We pronounce the final word, when we have neither reason nor right to. We cut a person down neatly with a word of criticism. To his face. Or behind his back. We nit-pick at someone else's behavior patterns and often fail to acknowledge our own weaknesses."[3]

Pride, self-centeredness and selfishness are keys to the lack of transparent relationships. "Selfishness, at its root, is self-protectiveness. Our primary commitment is to make certain no one can hurt us. The best way to do that is never to be fully vulnerable. An infant communicates helplessness without choosing to. His helplessness is obvious. As adults, we can hide how desperate we are for someone to care. Others won't clearly see our deepest needs unless we choose to make them known. The seed of self-protection is in the infant. In adults it's a full-grown weed."[4]

Numerous sociological factors also contribute to our lack of transparency. We live in an age of specialization. We either engage in "small talk" or "technicalities". We enjoy isolation after a busy day of work. We often are spectators rather than participants. We lack intergenerational interaction. All these factors coupled with pride, self-centeredness and selfishness wreak havoc on the experience of transparency.

Relating transparently to God and Others: The "How To's" and the "How Not To's" of Transparency

Our needs:
1. I need a relationship with a person *from whom I cannot hide*.
2. I need a relationship with a person *at whom I can hurl* but who gives me no cause to and will not be alienated if I do.
3. I need a relationship with a person *who will always tell me the truth*.

In short, I need a friend who knows me completely. God alone meets all of these requirements.[5]

Transparency with God grooms us for transparency with one another.

Being transparent involves a certain degree of not taking oneself too seriously. "The problems with taking ourselves too seriously are countless. Afraid to fail, we no longer risk. Afraid that someone will see behind our image, we no longer share. Afraid that we will appear to need help, we can no longer be vulnerable. Afraid to appear not religious enough to some, we no longer can confess. We withdraw into a petty world consumed in emptiness and fear, covered with a thick shell, worshipping an impotent God." [6]

To be transparent, we must be in touch with our communicational living channels. It is important to know if we respond best from the feeling, thinking, choosing or doing channels. Strong feelers are warm, very aware of emotions and effective in expressing them. In contrast, weak feelers are low in awareness and expression of emotions. Strong thinkers visualize actions and plans. Weak thinkers are impulsive and have difficulty seeing consequences. Strong choosers are decisive; life is charged with meaning. They have internalized moral standards, know their own values and demonstrate courage. Weak choosers are indecisive; their lives may lack meaning, clear moral standards, a value system or courage. Strong doers are active; they expend energy in action rather than worrying. Weak doers are immobilized; they spend much time daydreaming, fantasizing or feeling miserable.[7] How transparent you are will depend a great deal on your strongest and weakest living channels.

Scripture also gives us guidance regarding transparency. " Everyone should be quick to listen, slow to speak and slow to become angry" (James 1:19). Transparency involves both speaking and listening. Often it is as difficult for us to take in someone else's transparency as it is for us to be transparent. Because the brain is automatically self-protective, it tends to deceive itself daily from risking the pain of transparency "—weeping may remain for a night, but rejoicing comes in the morning" (Psalm 30:5b). Although a transparent interaction may be painful at the time, the benefits are long-lasting.

Defense mechanisms are frequent detours or roadblocks to transparency. They are ways we react to frustration and conflict by deceiving ourselves about our real desires and goals in an effort to maintain self-esteem and avoid anxiety. Common defense mechanisms include repression, denial, projection, rationalization, passive-aggressiveness, displacement and *phariseeism.*

Transparency takes place best in supportive settings. The type of support needed prescribes the support arena. When we need self-esteem, we desire transparency with people who know what we can do and are able to give us feedback. When we need personal connections, we desire transparent, intimate friends. Professional contacts provide work connection transparency. Social transparency takes place with people who are like us. Stimulation and challenge requires friendly kickers who push and stretch us. Role models are people we want to emulate. The transparency of a mentor helps

Relationship

navigate us to where we want to be. Spiritual directors encourage our spiritual strength and growth. Persons who are open and listen without criticism provide comfort and support vulnerability. Many forms of transparency and support are needed as we relate to others

Finally, transparency takes place best amongst "safe people."[8] A safe relationship does three things: draws us closer to God, to others, and helps us become the real person God created us to be. A safe person accepts us just as we are; loves us unconditionally; develops our ability to love and be responsible; gives us an opportunity to grow and allows us to be ourselves around them. They allow and help us become the people God intends. A safe person's life touches ours and leaves us better for it.

Why do we need safe, transparent relationships? For fuel, comfort, strength, encouragement, support, modeling, healing, confrontation, discipline, rooting, grounding and for love. Transparency is a critical bridge to God and to one another.

The Bridge of Transparency

Scriptural Insights:

The focus of these scriptural references is to give you a biblical understanding of the Bridge of Transparency. (Scriptures are printed in the back of the book.)

1. The scriptures below illustrate Jesus' transparency. What do you learn about Him in each of the passages? (Note parallel references are given when appropriate.)

   a. *Mt 8:20 (Lk 9:5 -8)*

   b. *Mt 9:2-8 (Mk 2: 3-12; Lk 5:18-26)*

   c. *Mt 12:25-29 (Mk 3: 23-27; Lk 11: 17-22)*

   d. *Mt 12: 46-50 (Mk 3: 31-34; Lk 8:19- 21)*

   e. *Mt 13:54-58 (Mk 6:1-6)*

   f. *Mt 16: 21-28 (Mk 8:31; Lk 9:2 2-27)*

   g. *Mt 17: 1-8 (Mk 9:2-13; Lk 9:28-36)*

   h. *Mt 22: 41-46 (Mk 12: 35-37; Lk 20: 41- 44)*

   i. *Mt 26: 6-13 (Mk 14:3-9; Lk 7 :37-38; Jn 12:1-8)*

   j. *Mt 26:17-29 (Mk 14:12-21; Lk 22:7-20)*

   k. *Mt 26:36-46 (Mk 14:32-42; Lk 22:40-46)*

   l. *Mt. 26: 63-64 (Mk 14: 57-62; Jn 12:19-24)*

   m. *Mt. 27: 11-13 (Mk 15:2-5; Lk 23:3; Jn 18:33-38)*

   n. *Mt 27:46 (Mk 15:34; Lk 23:46)*

   o. *Mt 28: 8-10*

2. In the Gospel of John, Jesus's transparency takes the form of seven "I Am"
statements. Who does Jesus say he is in each of the verses below:
    a. *Jn 6:35*
    b. *Jn 8:12*
    c. *Jn 8:58*
    d. *Jn 10:9, 14*
    e. *Jn 11:25*
    f. *Jn 14:6*
    g. *Jn 15:1*

3. *Pr. 20:5; Rom. 1:11-12; Jas. 5:16.*
What do these passages teach us about the benefits of transparency?

4. *Jos 7:7-9; Ps 25: 14 -15.*
How do these verses illustrate transparency between man and God?

The Bridge of Transparency

Focused Application:

"Everyone hears what you say. Friends listen to what you say. Best friends listen to what you don't say." —Unknown

I. What and who tends to keep you from being transparent? Explain.

II. Define in your own words, *hide* and *hurl*, the two antitheses of transparency. Give examples of each in your life.

III. What would you identify as Christ's most transparent moment? Why?

Describe several of your most transparent moments? What were the outcomes of being transparent?

IV. Which of the defense mechanisms below do you tend to use as a detour or roadblock to transparency? Give examples.

    a. repression
    b. denial
    c. projection
    d. rationalization
    e. passive-aggressiveness
    f. displacement
    g. *phariseeism*

Make a commitment to catch yourself in the act of employing this (these) defense mechanisms so that you can move to eliminating them from you life.

V. Who are the *safe* people in your life?

VI. Below is a list of the potential needs in our lives. Who in your life provides support and the opportunity for transparency in each of these areas:

Need	*Type of Support*	*Who In My Life Provides this Support*
Self-esteem	People who know what you can do	
Personal connections	Intimate friends	
Work connections	Professional contacts	
Social connections	People who like you	
Peer	People who are like you	
Stimulation and challenge	'Friendly kicker,' pushes and stretches	
Role models	People you want to emulate	

Navigation—how to get where you want	Mentor or sponsor
Spiritual	Sources of spiritual strength and growth
Security	People who meet survival needs
Comfort and vulnerability	People who are 'open' listen without criticism

CHAPTER 16

The Bridge of Trust

Key Scripture: By awesome deeds in righteousness you will answer us, O God of our salvation, you who are the confidence (trust) of all the ends of the earth. Psalm 65:5a

Overview:

Trust is a primary ingredient in the making of a relationship. This includes both our relationships with God and with each other. Trust is a foundational beam that keeps us connected to God. In turn, we determine to be trustworthy people in order to stay connected with others. The bridge of trust is built upon the confidence we have in God and who we are positionally in Jesus Christ. Unless we are firm in our belief of God's unchanging love for us, and that His ways are good and righteous, we cannot wholly trust Him with our decisions—or our lives. The degree to which we know and believe in God's character is the degree to which we can and will trust Him.

The "Bridge of Trust" study guide addresses the following:

- The foundation of a solid structure—trusting God
- How trust builds a relationship
- The two sides of trust

Relationship

Scriptural references throughout provide biblical support for the bridge.

The "Focused Application" segment allows you to apply the scriptural principles addressed in "Core Concepts" and "Scriptural Insights".

Core Concepts:

Author Linda Dillow, in her article, "Why Should I Trust God?" speaks of Amy Carmichael, missionary to India's children. Amy Carmichael said that her ability to trust God began with her confidence in God's character. She believed that God is, first and always, a loving Father. She believed that God was in control, and everything He allowed into her life was ultimately for her good. And as she "tucked herself into God" by trusting Him as a little child, she believed He was able to carry her through all things. [1]

The foundation of a solid structure—trusting God:

In order to trust that God is in control, we have to trust that He is sovereign. We have to see Him as the loving and blessed only Ruler. 1Timothy 6:15 says, "Which God will bring about in His own time God, the blessed and only Ruler, the King of Kings and Lord of Lords." God is in control of all that is uncontrollable in our lives: what we can not see, what does not make sense to us, what we do not understand. "Are not two sparrows sold for a penny? Yet not one of them will fall to the ground apart from the will of your Father. And even the very hairs of your head are all numbered. So do not be afraid; you are worth more than many sparrows" (Matthew 10: 29-31). Jesus was teaching that God providentially controls the timing and circumstances of such insignificant events as the death of a sparrow. Even the number of hairs on our heads is controlled by His sovereign will. In other words, divine providence governs even the smallest details and most mundane matters. These are very powerful affirmations of the sovereignty of God. There are no accidents, no mistakes, and no miscalculations. All is under His sovereign control. In our relationship with God, we often find ourselves not believing what we say we believe, especially during

The Bridge of Trust

the difficult times in our lives. We find ourselves clinging shakily to scriptural truths, truths directly challenged by apparent reality. Therefore, we must be diligent to believe what we already know, believe in the deepest places of our hearts, this truth foundational to our faith—the sovereignty of God.

In our journey to trust God, it helps to know and believe that He is sovereign. It also helps to know that He is wise. The Hebrew word used in the scriptures for wisdom means 'skill'. Applied to God, it means that He has the skill necessary to conceptualize the best possible course of action for running the world. He knows everything about us. He knows the best plan for our lives. "For I know the plans I have for you, declares the Lord. Plans to prosper you and not to harm you, plans to give you hope and a future" (Jeremiah 29:11). We see from this scripture that God is actively laying plans for His people. According to Solomon, "By wisdom the Lord laid the earth's foundations; by understanding He set the heavens in place" (Proverbs 3:19). The writer here is indicating that wisdom is basic to all of life, for by it God created everything. This being so, we can trust God, knowing that everything that happens to us is thought out by an infinitely wise Person, one wise enough to found the earth and establish the heavens. God's wisdom means that He allows circumstances to occur in our lives for His purposes and for our highest good. Do we understand why? No. Our wisdom is inferior to God's. When we trust His wisdom, we are able to grow into a deeper relationship with Him.

To trust God we must also trust His love. We can know intellectually that God is love, but for trust to flourish we must also be able to personalize His love for us on a daily basis. According to Deuteronomy 31:7-8 "Then Moses called Joshua and said to him in the sight of all Israel, Be strong and of good courage, for you must go with this people to the land which the Lord has sworn to their fathers to give them, and you shall cause them to inherit it. And the Lord, He is the One who goes before you. He will be with you; do not fear nor be dismayed." The strength and courage of the warriors of Israel would come from their confidence that their God was with them and would not forsake them. "The Lord has appeared of old to me saying: Yes, I have loved you with an everlasting love; therefore with loving-kindness I have drawn you" (Jeremiah 31:3). Paul understands this principle of love very well. "Who shall separate us from the love of Christ? Shall tribulation, or distress, or persecution, or famine, or nakedness, or peril, or sword? Yet in all these things we are more than conquerors through Him who loved us. For I am persuaded that neither death nor life, nor angels nor principalities, nor powers, nor things present nor things to come, nor height nor depth, nor any other created thing, shall be able to separate us from the love of God which is in Christ Jesus our Lord" (Romans 8: 35-39). The list of experiences and persons that cannot separate the believer from God's love in Christ was not just theory to the apostle Paul. It was, rather, a personal testimony from one who had personally survived assaults from these entities and emerged triumphantly. Paul is saying, in more common terms, adversities, being hemmed in by difficult circumstances that can make us feel helpless, suffering persecution because of our relationship with Christ, cannot separate us from victorious living found in Christ. Nothing can separate us from His watchful eye and constant love. The Bible proclaims the profound truth that "God works all things together for good for those who love Him and are called according to His purpose" (Romans 8: 28). The definition of *good* follows: "For those God foreknew He also predestined to be conformed to the likeness of His Son" (Romans 8:29). Whatever comes into our lives is *good* because it is making us more like Christ. God promises that there is a purpose for difficult circumstances. It is good because as we grow to trust Him with our pains and pressures, our character will become more like His. Why should we trust God? Because He is trustworthy. He deserves our trust. When we trust Him, we participate in purposes and plans that transcend our own. As author Larry Crabb explains, "A commitment to trust the Lord deeply with the core of our being can turn every emotion, even the most painful, into constructive avenues for more fully pursuing God." [2]

How trust builds a relationship:

Because many of us only half-heartedly believe who the Bible says we are in Christ, we live 'half-effective' lives—defeated more often

than victorious in our relationships. We can unintentionally discount what scripture says about us as new creatures in Christ.
- That we are the righteousness of God in Christ — 2 Corinthians 5: 21.
- That we are free from condemnation — Romans 8: 1.
- That we are fearfully and wonderfully made — Psalm 139: 14.
- That God is for me — Romans 8: 31

Yet what we believe about ourselves directly influences how we relate to others. Trust builds a relationship. In order to develop trust we must remember who we are in Christ. To be more committed to self-protection than relating to each other the way God intended is sin, which is missing the target that God has set up as His standard for us to live. Developing trust in a relationship involves remembering who we are in Christ, but it also involves remembering how we are to live as followers of Christ. As Disciples of Christ, we are to be prudent in our relating to others, yet vulnerable. Our Master lived out servanthood. We are to trust God, which will allow us to trust others. Trust builds a relationship because it says to the other person, " I value you. I believe you are worthy of my trust". There is a strong belief that you are for one another, not against each other. Trust builds a relationship because confidence becomes a noted characteristic. People can rely on one another. Interdependence grows out of trusting one another.

The two sides of trust:

John Maxwell, the leadership expert and noted author, makes the case for trust in his book *The 21 Irrefutable Laws of Leadership.* "When I think of leaders who epitomize consistency of character, the first person who comes to mind is Billy Graham. Regardless of personal religious beliefs, everybody trusts him. Why? Because he has modeled high character for more than half a century. He lives out his values every day. He never makes a commitment unless he is going to keep it. And he goes out of his way to personify integrity."[3] Trust has to be earned. For someone to trust us, we must be trustworthy. Being trustworthy involves many facets of solid character.

Relationship

John Maxwell cites the following reasons why Billy Graham is trusted:
- Consistency of character—making daily decisions based upon convictions of belief rather than momentary feelings
- Modeling integrity—practically applying the biblical truths we say we believe
- Keeping commitments—a commitment is a weighty promise to be taken seriously

Clearly, one side of developing trust in a relationship is for both people to be trustworthy. It is impossible to build a bridge of trust without living lives that are founded on Godly character.

The other side of developing trust in a relationship involves confronting the insecurities we all possess. The fact is we all have been rejected, possibly abandoned, to some degree in our lives. We have all received wounds of varying descriptions from others. Often our most significant relations—parents, siblings, mates and close friends—have inflicted these wounds upon us. Trust, therefore, becomes a huge obstacle to overcome. In order to build the bridge of trust we must actively labor through the process of seeing God heal our damaged emotions. This is a prerequisite for building trust in a relationship.

Trust is a powerful experience. We begin by trusting God through Christ. Trust will continue to build as we recognize and live in the glorious reality of who we are in Christ. As we practice these truths, trust will begin to emerge between others and ourselves.

Scriptural Insights:

The focus of these scriptural references is to give you a biblical understanding of the "Bridge of Trust".

1. According to *Ps 65:5* who is the true object of our trust?

2. *Isa 26:4*
Na 1:7
Ps 36:7
1 Tim 6:17
1 Pe 5:7
Ps 9:10, 2 Co 1:10
These scriptures encourage us to place our trust in God. Each reference has one reason for placing our trust in God. What are those reasons?

3. *Ps 5:11; 32:10; 37:5; 37:40; 125:1*
Pr 16:20; 28:25; 29:25
Isa 26:3; 57:13
What are the results of trusting God according to these scriptures?

Focused Application:

I. How would you describe God?

II. Using your description of God, would it be easy for you to trust Him?

III. Rate your trust level of God on a scale from 1 to 10.

Lowest trust   Highest trust

IV. Is God fair? Have you experienced times when you doubted God's wisdom? Has God let you down? Explain. Now ask yourself, was it God letting me down, or did I assume that I knew what was best for me in the situation?

V. Do you believe that God is sovereign? What causes you to doubt His sovereignty? Do you believe that God knows everything?

VI. Do you feel that you are expected to 'map out' your life's plans or do you consider that God's responsibility? Write briefly about a time in your life when you attempted to arrange things. What happened?

VII. Do you believe God loves you? How do you know?

VIII. Is it easy for you to trust others? Why or why not?

IX. Do you consider yourself a trustworthy person? What character traits might be missing that keeps others from trusting you?

X. Do you struggle with any insecurity that makes trusting God or others a difficulty?

XI. Who are you putting your trust in right now? Why?

Building Bridges

A STORY

Once upon a time two brothers who lived on adjoining farms fell into conflict. It was the first serious rift in 40 years of farming side by side, sharing machinery, and trading labor and goods as needed without a hitch. Then the long collaboration fell apart. It began with a small misunderstanding and it grew into a major difference, and finally it exploded into an exchange of bitter words followed by weeks of silence.

One morning there was a knock on John's door. He opened it to find a man with a carpenter's toolbox. "I'm looking for a few days work," he said. "Perhaps you would have a few small jobs here and there I could help with? Could I help you?" "Yes," said the older brother. "I do have a job for you. Look across the creek at that farm. That's my neighbor, in fact, it's my younger brother. Last week there was a meadow between us and he took his bulldozer to the river levee and now there is a creek between us. Well, he may have done this to spite me, but I'll do him one better. See that pile of lumber by the barn? I want you to build me a fence — an 8-foot fence — so I won't need to see his place or his face anymore."

The carpenter said, "I think I understand the situation. Show me the nails and the post-hole digger and I'll be able to do a job that pleases you." The older brother had to go to town, so he helped the carpenter get the materials ready and then he was off for the day.

Relationship

The carpenter worked hard all that day measuring, sawing, and nailing.

About sunset when the farmer returned, the carpenter had just finished his job. The farmer's eyes opened wide, his jaw dropped. There was no fence there at all. It was a bridge — a bridge stretching from one side of the creek to the other! A fine piece of work handrails and all — and the neighbor, his younger brother, was coming across, his hand outstretched. "You are quite a fellow to build this bridge after all I've said and done." The two brothers stood at each end of the bridge, and then they met in the middle, taking each other's hand. They turned to see the carpenter hoist his toolbox on his shoulder. "No, wait! Stay a few days. I've a lot of other projects for you," said the older brother. "I'd love to stay on," the carpenter said, "but, I have many more bridges to build."

—Author Unknown

Notes

Introduction
[1] Max Lucado, *On the Anvil: Stories On Being Shaped Into God's Image* (Wheaton, Ill: Tyndale House, 1985), 67-70. Used by permission.

Chapter 1 Our Foundation: Life in Christ
[1] Billy Graham, *How to be Born Again* (Waco, TX: Word Publishing, 1977), 150-151. Used by permission.
[2] Robert S. McGee, *The Search for Significance* (Houston, TX: Rapha Publishing, 1987), 25. Used by permission.
[3] Larry Crabb, *Connecting* (Nashville, TN: Word Publishing, 1997), xvi. Used by permission.

Chapter 2 The Bridge of Authenticity
[1] M. Scott Peck, *Different Drum* (New York, NY: Simon & Schuster, 1987).
[2] Bill Hybels, *Authenticity* (Grand Rapids, MI: Zondervan Publishing House, 1996). Used by permission.
[3] Eugene Peterson, *Run With the Horses* (Downers Grove, Il: InterVarsity Press, 1983), 16. Used by permission.
[4] Richard Swenson, *Hurtling Toward Oblivion* (Colorado Springs, CO: NavPress, 1999), 122-123. Used by permission.
[5] Larry Crabb, *The Safety Place on Earth* (Nashville, TN: Word Publishing, 1999), 117. Used by permission.
[6] Geoff Safford, *Pastoral Message* (Minneapolis, MN: Crystal Evangelical Free Church, Apr 2, 1998).
[7] Bill Hybels, *Authenticity* (Grand Rapids, MI: Zondervan Publishing House, 1996), 11-18, 58. Used by permission.
[8] Paul Welter, *How to Help a Friend* (Wheaton, Il: Tyndale House Publishers, 1974), 88-89.

Relationship

Chapter 3 The Bridge of Communication
None

Chapter 4 The Bridge of Compassion
[1] Charles Swindoll, *Compassion: Showing Care in a Careless World* (Waco, TX: Word Publishing, 1984), 11, 39. Used by permission.
[2] Spiros Zodhiates, Th.D., *The Complete Word Study Dictionary* (Chattanooga, TN: AMG Publishers, 1992), 1306.
[3] Don & Katie Fortune, *Discover Your God-Given Gifts* (Grand Rapids, MI: Baker Book House, 1987), 181-201.
[4] James Strong, *Strong's Exhaustive Concordance of the Bible* (New York: Abingdon Press, 1970) as quoted in *Discover Your God Given Gifts*.
[5] David Stevens, M.D., *Jesus M.D.: A Doctor Examines the Great Physician* (Grand Rapids, MI: Zondervan Publishing House, 2001), 177; 180-182. Used by permission.

Chapter 5 The Bridge of Contentment
[1] Larry Crabb, *Shattered Dreams* (Colorado Springs, CO: WaterBrook Press, 2001), 70. Used by permission.
[2] Ibid., 2. Used by permission.
[3] Ibid., 86. Used by permission.
[4] Larry Crabb, *Inside Out* (Colorado Springs, CO: Navpress, 1988), 87-88. Used by permission.
[5] Tim Hansel, *When I Relax I Feel Guilty* (Elgin, Ill.: David C. Cook Publishing Co, 1981), 80-87. Used by permission.

Chapter 6 The Bridge of Forgiveness
[1] Robert Jeffress, *When Forgiveness Doesn't Make Sense* (Colorado Springs, CO: Waterbrook Press, 2000). Used by permission.
[2] Kathy E. Dahlen "Free to Forgive" *Discipleship Journal* (Colorado Springs, CO: 1998, Issue 105). Used by permission.
[3] Bob Moorehead *Counsel Yourself & Others from the Bible* (Sisters, OR: Multnomah Books, 1994), 70-71. Used by permission.

Chapter 7 The Bridge of Grace
[1] Thomas A Kempis, *Imitation of Christ* (Nashville, TN: Thomas Nelson Publishers, 1999), 47.
[2] Max Lucado, *In The Grip of Grace* (Dallas, TX: Word Publishing, 1996), 107. Used by permission.

Chapter 8 The Bridge of Hope
[1] C.S. Lewis, "Hope" excerpt from *Mere Christianity* in *The Joyful Christian: 127 Readings* (New York, NY: Simon & Schuster, 1977), 138. Used by permission.
[2] John Ortberg, *If you Want to Walk on Water, You've Got to Get Out of the Boat* (Grand Rapids, MI: Zondervan Publishing House, 2001), 157. Used by permission.

Notes

³ David Henderson, *"Hope: Anchoring Your Heart to a Sure and Certain Future" Discipleship Journal* (Colorado Springs, CO: NavPress, Issue 114, 1999), 53-56.

⁴ Max Lucado, *God Came Near: Chronicles of the Christ* (Portland, OR: Multnomah Press, 1987), 89. Used by permission.

⁵ Daniel Goleman, *Emotional Intelligence* (New York, NY: Bantam Books, 1995), 87. Used by permission.

⁶ William Buchholz, M.D., *"Hope"* in *Chicken Soup for the Surviving Soul* (Deerfield Beach, Fl: Health Communications, Inc., 1996), 21.

⁷ John Ortberg, *If you Want to Walk on Water, You've Got to Get Out of the Boat* (Grand Rapids, MI: Zondervan Publishing House, 2001), 155. Used by permission.

⁸ Ibid., 161. Used by permission.

⁹ David Henderson, "Hope: Anchoring Your Heart to a Sure and Certain Future" Discipleship Journal (Colorado Springs, CO: NavPress, Issue 114, 1999), 55.

Chapter 9 The Bridge of Hospitality

¹ Eleanor L. Doan, *The Speaker's Sourcebook* (Grand Rapids, MI: Zondervan Publishing House, 1977), 200. Used by permission.

² Karen Burton Mains, *Open Heart, Open Home* (Elgin, IL: David C. Cook Publishing Co, 1976), 24. Used by permission.

³ Stephen W. Sorenson, "No Place Like Home" *Discipleship Journal* (Colorado Springs, CO: NavPress, 1999, Issue 114), 88. Used by permission.

⁴ Elizabeth George, *A Woman's High Calling* (Eugene, OR: Harvest House Publishers, 2001), 258-259. Used by permission.

⁵ Ken Gire, *Windows of the Soul* (Grand Rapids, MI: Zondervan Publishing House, 1996), 52. Used by permission.

Chapter 10 The Bridge of Impartiality

¹ Charles Swindol, *Christ At The Crossroads* (Anaheim, CA: Insight for Living, 1998) 113.

² Donald W. Burdick, "James" in the Expositor's Bible Commentary, ed. Frank E. Gasbelein *Sourcebook* (Grand Rapids, MI: Zondervan Publishing House, 1981), vol. 12, 180. Used by permission.

³ C.S. Lewis, *The Weight of Glory* (New York , NY: Macmillan Publishing Co., 1980), 19.

⁴ David A. Rausch, A Legacy of Hatred: Why Christians Must Not Forget the Holocaust (Grand Rapids, MI: Baker Book House, 1990), 5. Used by permission.

Chapter 11 The Bridge of Integrity

¹ C.S. Lewis, "Virtue" excerpt from *Mere Christianity* in *The Joyful Christian: 127 Readings* (New York , NY: Simon & Schuster, 1977) 124. Used by permission.

² Jerry White, "The Power of Integrity" *Discipleship Journal* (Colorado Springs, CO: NavPress, Issue 104), as cited by Michael M. Smith in *Character: Becoming More Like Jesus* (Colorado Springs, CO: NavPress, 1999) 33-35. Used by permission.

³ Carolyn Nystrom, *Integrity: Living the Truth 10 Studies for Individuals or Groups* (Downers Grove, Ill: InterVarsity Press, 2000) 4. Used by permission.

⁴ Charles Swindol, Ken Gire and Gary Matlock, *Strengthening Your Grip Bible Study Guide* (Dallas, TX: Word Publishing, 1995) 38-42. Used by permission.

5 Thomas Carylyle, as quoted in *Bartlett's Familiar Quotations*, 15th ed., rev. and enl., ed. Emily Morison Beck (Boston, Mass.: Little, Brown and Co., 1980), 474.

Chapter 12 The Bridge of Intimacy

1. Erik Erikson, *Identity, Youth and Crises* (New York, NY: W.W. Norton, 1968), 168-169.

Chapter 13 The Bridge of Love

1 Larry Crabb, *Understanding People* (Grand Rapids, MI: Zondervan Publishing House, 1987), 196-197. Used by permission.

2 C. S. Lewis, *The Four Loves* (New York, NY: Harcourt Brace Jovanovich William Collins Sons and Co., 1960), 169.

3 Larry Crabb, *Understanding People* (Grand Rapids, MI: Zondervan Publishing House, 1987), 199. Used by permission.

Chapter 14 The Bridge of Prayer

1 Ruth Harms Calkin in *The One Year Book of Personal Prayer* (Wheaton, Ill: Tyndale House Publishers, 1991), 57.

2 As quoted by J. Oswald Sanders in *Spiritual Leadership*, rev. ed. (Chicago, Ill.: Moody Press, 1980), 103. Used by permission.

3 Bill Hybels, *Prayer* (Grand Rapids, MI: Zondervan Publishing House, 1997), 11; 14, 23-27, 31. Used by permission.

4 Richard Foster, *Prayers: Finding the Heart's True Home* (San Francisco, CA: Harper San Francisco, 1992), viii-xii.

5 T.W. Hunt & Catherine Walker, *Disciple's Prayer Life* (Nashville, TN: Life Way Press, 1997), 10. Used by permission.

6 Ibid., 214. Used by permission.

7 Charles R. Swindoll, *Hand Me Another Brick: A Study of Nehemiah Bible Study Guide* (Dallas, TX: Word Publishing, 1990), 84-89. Used by permission.

8 Brenda Poinsett, "What Jesus Taught Me About Prayer" *Discipleship Journal* (Colorado Springs, CO: NavPress, 1999, Issue 114), 78-83. Used by permission.

9 Nancy Nordenson, "Praying When Life Gets Hard" *Discipleship Journal* (Colorado Springs, CO: NavPress, 2000, Issue 116), 32-37. Used by permission.

10 Paul Borthwick, "In Jesus' Name" *Discipleship Journal* (Colorado Springs, CO: NavPress, 2000, Issue 117), 86-89. Used by permission.

11 *The One Year Book of Personal Prayer* (Wheaton, Ill: Tyndale House Publishers, 1991), 42.

12 Henri J. M. Nouwen *Sabbatical Journey* (New York, NY: Crossroad Publishing Co, 1998), 5-6.

Chapter 15 The Bridge of Transparency

1 J. Grant Howard, *The Trauma of Transparency* (Portland, OR: Multnomah Press, 1979), 219. Used by permission.

2 Bill Hybels, *Transparency* (Grand Rapids, MI: Zondervan Publishing House, 1997), back cover. Used by permission.

3 Ibid., 27; 32. Used by permission.

[4] Larry Crabb, *Shattered Dreams* (Colorado Springs, CO: WaterBrook Press, 2001), 18. Used by permission.

[5] J. Grant Howard, *The Trauma of Transparency* Portland, OR: Multnomah Press, 1979), 70. Used by permission.

[6] Tim Hansel, *When I Relax I Feel Guilty* (Elgin, Ill.: David C. Cook Publishing Co, 1981), 87. Used by permission.

[7] Paul Welter, *How to Help a Friend* (Wheaton, Il: Tyndale House Publishers, 1974), 88-89; 96-97.

[8] Henry Cloud & John Townsend, *Safe People* (Grand Rapid, MI: Zondervan Publishing House, 1995. Used by permission.

Chapter 16 The Bridge of Trust

[1] Linda Dillow, "Why Should I Trust God?" *Discipleship Journal* (Colorado Springs, CO: NavPress, 1998, Issue 103), frame 2.

[2] Lawrence J. Crabb, Jr., *Understanding People* (Grand Rapids, MI: Zondervan Publishing House, 1987), 183. Used by permission.

[3] John C. Maxwell, *The 21 Irrefutable Laws of Leadership* (Nashville, TN: Thomas Nelson Publishers, 1998), 59.

Scripture References

Chapter 1: Our Foundation: The Life in Christ Scriptures

Jn 1:12 Yet to all who received him, to those who believed in his name, he gave the right to become children of God

Eph 1:4 For he chose us in him before the creation of the world to be holy and blameless in his sight. In love 5 he predestined us to be adopted as his sons through Jesus Christ, in accordance with his pleasure and will— 6 to the praise of his glorious grace, which he has freely given us in the One he loves. 7 In him we have redemption through his blood, the forgiveness of sins, in accordance with the riches of God's grace

Eph 2:8 For it is by grace you have been saved, through faith—and this not from yourselves, it is the gift of God— 9 not by works, so that no one can boast. 10 For we are God's workmanship, created in Christ Jesus to do good works, which God prepared in advance for us to do.

1 Pe 1:18 For you know that it was not with perishable things such as silver or gold that you were redeemed from the empty way of life handed down to you from your forefathers, 19 but with the precious blood of Christ, a lamb without blemish or defect.

Jn 3:3 In reply Jesus declared, "I tell you the truth, no one can see the kingdom of God unless he is born again." 4 "How can a man be born when he is old?" Nicodemus asked. "Surely he cannot enter a second time into his mother's womb to be born!" 5 Jesus answered, "I tell you the truth, no one can enter the kingdom of God unless he is born of water and the Spirit. 6 Flesh gives birth to flesh, but the

Spirit gives birth to spirit. 7 You should not be surprised at my saying, 'You must be born again.' 8 The wind blows wherever it pleases. You hear its sound, but you cannot tell where it comes from or where it is going. So it is with everyone born of the Spirit."

Tit 3:5 he saved us, not because of righteous things we had done, but because of his mercy. He saved us through the washing of rebirth and renewal by the Holy Spirit,

Lk 13:3 But unless you repent, you too will all perish.

Ac 2:38 Peter replied, "Repent and be baptized, every one of you, in the name of Jesus Christ for the forgiveness of your sins. And you will receive the gift of the Holy Spirit.

Ac 3:19 Repent, then, and turn to God, so that your sins may be wiped out, that times of refreshing may come from the Lord

Ac 11:18 When they heard this, they had no further objections and praised God, saying, "So then, God has granted even the Gentiles repentance unto life."

Ac 20:32 "Now I commit you to God and to the word of his grace, which can build you up and give you an inheritance among all those who are sanctified.

1 Cor 1:2 To the church of God in Corinth, to those sanctified in Christ Jesus and called to be holy, together with all those everywhere who call on the name of our Lord Jesus Christ—their Lord and ours:

1 Cor 1:30 It is because of him that you are in Christ Jesus, who has become for us wisdom from God—that is, our righteousness, holiness and redemption.

1 Cor 6:11 And that is what some of you were. But you were washed, you were sanctified, you were justified in the name of the Lord Jesus Christ and by the Spirit of our God.

Heb 2:11 Both the one who makes men holy and those who are made holy are of the same family. So Jesus is not ashamed to call them brothers.

Heb 3:1 Therefore, holy brothers, who share in the heavenly calling, fix your thoughts on Jesus, the apostle and high priest whom we confess.

Chapter 2: The Bridge of Authenticity Scriptures

2 Cor 10:7 You are looking only on the surface of things. If anyone is confident that he belongs to Christ, he should consider again that we belong to Christ just as much as he.

Da 2:1 In the second year of his reign, Nebuchadnezzar had dreams; his mind was troubled and he could not sleep. 2 So the king summoned the magicians, enchanters, sorcerers and astrologers to tell him what he had dreamed. When they came in and stood before the king, 3 he said to them, "I have had a dream that troubles me and I want to know what it means. " 4 Then the astrologers answered the king in Aramaic, "O king, live forever! Tell your servants the dream, and we will interpret it." 5 The king replied to the astrologers, "This is what I have firmly decided: If you do not tell me what my dream was and interpret it, I will have you cut into pieces and your houses turned into piles of rubble. 6 But if you tell me the dream and explain it, you will receive from me gifts and rewards and great honor. So tell me the dream and interpret it for me." 7 Once more they replied, "Let the king tell his servants the dream, and we will interpret it." 8 Then the king answered, "I am certain that you are trying to gain time, because you realize that this is what I have firmly decided: 9 If you do not tell me the dream, there is just one penalty for you. You have conspired to tell me misleading and wicked things, hoping the situation will change. So then, tell me the dream, and I will know that you can interpret it for me." 10 The astrologers answered the king, "There is not a man on earth who can do what the king asks! No king, however great and mighty, has ever asked such a thing of any magician or enchanter or astrologer. 11 What the king asks is too difficult. No one can reveal it to the king except the gods, and they do not live among men."

Mt 3:1 In those days John the Baptist came, preaching in the Desert of Judea 2 and saying, "Repent, for the kingdom of heaven is near." 3 This is he who was spoken of through the prophet Isaiah: "A voice of one calling in the desert, 'Prepare the way for the Lord, make straight paths for him.'" 4 John's clothes were made of camel's hair, and he had a leather belt around his waist. His food was locusts and wild honey. 5 People went out to him from Jerusalem and all Judea and the whole region of the Jordan. 6

Confessing their sins, they were baptized by him in the Jordan River. 7 But when he saw many of the Pharisees and Sadducees coming to where he was baptizing, he said to them: "You brood of vipers! Who warned you to flee from the coming wrath? 8 Produce fruit in keeping with repentance. 9 And do not think you can say to yourselves, 'We have Abraham as our father.' I tell you that out of these stones God can raise up children for Abraham. 10 The ax is already at the root of the trees, and every tree that does not produce good fruit will be cut down and thrown into the fire. 11 "I baptize you with water for repentance. But after me will come one who is more powerful than I, whose sandals I am not fit to carry. He will baptize you with the Holy Spirit and with fire.

Mt 11:1 After Jesus had finished instructing his twelve disciples, he went on from there to teach and preach in the towns of Galilee. 2 When John heard in prison what Christ was doing, he sent his disciples 3 to ask him, "Are you the one who was to come, or should we expect someone else?" 4 Jesus replied, "Go back and report to John what you hear and see: 5 The blind receive sight, the lame walk, those who have leprosy are cured, the deaf hear, the dead are raised, and the good news is preached to the poor. 6 Blessed is the man who does not fall away on account of me." 7 As John's disciples were leaving, Jesus began to speak to the crowd about John: "What did you go out into the desert to see? A reed swayed by the wind? 8 If not, what did you go out to see? A man dressed in fine clothes? No, those who wear fine clothes are in kings' palaces. 9 Then what did you go out to see? A prophet? Yes, I tell you, and more than a prophet. 10 This is the one about whom it is written: "'I will send my messenger ahead of you, who will prepare your way before you.' 11 I tell you the truth: Among those born of women there has not risen anyone greater than John the Baptist; yet he who is least in the kingdom of heaven is greater than he. 12 From the days of John the Baptist until now, the kingdom of heaven has been forcefully advancing, and forceful men lay hold of it. 13 For all the Prophets and the Law prophesied until John. 14 And if you are willing to accept it, he is the Elijah who was to come. 15 He who has ears, let him hear.

Jn 3:21 But whoever lives by the truth comes into the light, so that it may be seen plainly that what he has done has been done through God.

Ac 26-27 When he came to Jerusalem, he tried to join the disciples, but they were all afraid of him, not believing that he really was a disciple. 27 But Barnabas took him and brought him to the apostles. He told them how Saul on his journey had seen the Lord and that the Lord had spoken to him, and how in Damascus he had preached fearlessly in the name of Jesus.
Eph 4:23 to be made new in the attitude of your minds; 24 and to put on the new self, created to be like God in true righteousness and holiness. 25 Therefore each of you must put off falsehood and speak truthfully to his neighbor, for we are all members of one body. 26 "In your anger do not sin": Do not let the sun go down while you are still angry,
Php 4:8 Finally, brothers, whatever is true, whatever is noble, whatever is right, whatever is pure, whatever is lovely, whatever is admirable—if anything is excellent or praiseworthy—think about such things.
Mt 6:33 But seek first his kingdom and his righteousness, and all these things will be given to you as well.
Jer 17:9 The heart is deceitful above all things and beyond cure. Who can understand it? 10 "I the LORD search the heart and examine the mind, to reward a man according to his conduct, according to what his deeds deserve."
1 Sa 16:7 But the LORD said to Samuel, "Do not consider his appearance or his height, for I have rejected him. The LORD does not look at the things man looks at. Man looks at the outward appearance, but the LORD looks at the heart."

Chapter 3: The Bridge of Communication Scriptures

Jas 1:19 My dear brothers, take note of this: Everyone should be quick to listen, slow to speak and slow to become angry,
Pr 15:1 A gentle answer turns away wrath, but a harsh word stirs up anger.
Eph 4:26 "In your anger do not sin": Do not let the sun go down while you are still angry,
Ecc 12:10 The Teacher searched to find just the right words, and what he wrote was upright and true.
Pr 16:24 Pleasant words are a honeycomb, sweet to the soul and

Relationship

healing to the bones.

Pr 25:11 A word aptly spoken is like apples of gold in settings of silver.

Isa 50:4 The Sovereign LORD has given me an instructed tongue, to know the word that sustains the weary. He wakens me morning by morning, wakens my ear to listen like one being taught.

Col 4:6 Let your conversation be always full of grace, seasoned with salt, so that you may know how to answer everyone.

Jas 3:1 Not many of you should presume to be teachers, my brothers, because you know that we who teach will be judged more strictly. 2 We all stumble in many ways. If anyone is never at fault in what he says, he is a perfect man, able to keep his whole body in check. 3 When we put bits into the mouths of horses to make them obey us, we can turn the whole animal. 4 Or take ships as an example. Although they are so large and are driven by strong winds, they are steered by a very small rudder wherever the pilot wants to go. 5 Likewise the tongue is a small part of the body, but it makes great boasts. Consider what a great forest is set on fire by a small spark. 6 The tongue also is a fire, a world of evil among the parts of the body. It corrupts the whole person, sets the whole course of his life on fire, and is itself set on fire by hell. 7 All kinds of animals, birds, reptiles and creatures of the sea are being tamed and have been tamed by man, 8 but no man can tame the tongue. It is a restless evil, full of deadly poison. 9 With the tongue we praise our Lord and Father, and with it we curse men, who have been made in God's likeness. 10 Out of the same mouth come praise and cursing. My brothers, this should not be. 11 Can both fresh water and salt water flow from the same spring? 12 My brothers, can a fig tree bear olives, or a grapevine bear figs? Neither can a salt spring produce fresh water. 13 Who is wise and understanding among you? Let him show it by his good life, by deeds done in the humility that comes from wisdom. 14 But if you harbor bitter envy and selfish ambition in your hearts, do not boast about it or deny the truth. 15 Such "wisdom" does not come down from heaven but is earthly, unspiritual, of the devil. 16 For where you have envy and selfish ambition, there you find disorder and every evil practice. 17 But the wisdom that comes from heaven is first of all pure; then peace-loving, considerate, submissive, full of mercy and good fruit, impartial and sincere. 18 Peacemakers who sow in peace raise a harvest of righteousness.

Chapter 4: The Bridge of Compassion Scriptures

Isa 56:6 And foreigners who bind themselves to the LORD to serve him, to love the name of the LORD, and to worship him, all who keep the Sabbath without desecrating it and who hold fast to my covenant— 7 these I will bring to my holy mountain and give them joy in my house of prayer. Their burnt offerings and sacrifices will be accepted on my altar; for my house will be called a house of prayer for all nations." 8 The Sovereign LORD declares— he who gathers the exiles of Israel: "I will gather still others to them besides those already gathered." 9 Come, all you beasts of the field, come and devour, all you beasts of the forest! 10 Israel's watchmen are blind, they all lack knowledge; they are all mute dogs, they cannot bark; they lie around and dream, they love to sleep. 11 They are dogs with mighty appetites; they never have enough. They are shepherds who lack understanding; they all turn to their own way, each seeks his own gain. 12 "Come," each one cries, "let me get wine! Let us drink our fill of beer! And tomorrow will be like today, or even far better."

Dt 30:3 then the LORD your God will restore your fortunes and have compassion on you and gather you again from all the nations where he scattered you.

Dt 32:36 The LORD will judge his people and have compassion on his servants when he sees their strength is gone and no one is left, slave or free.

Ne 9:17 They refused to listen and failed to remember the miracles you performed among them. They became stiff-necked and in their rebellion appointed a leader in order to return to their slavery. But you are a forgiving God, gracious and compassionate, slow to anger and abounding in love. Therefore you did not desert them,

Ps 51:1 Have mercy on me, O God, according to your unfailing love; according to your great compassion blot out my transgressions.

Ps 86:15 But you, O Lord, are a compassionate and gracious God, slow to anger, abounding in love and faithfulness.

Relationship

Ps 103:13 As a father has compassion on his children, so the LORD has compassion on those who fear him;
Ps 119:156 Your compassion is great, O LORD; preserve my life according to your laws.
Ps 145:9 The LORD is good to all; he has compassion on all he has made.
Isa 30:18 Yet the LORD longs to be gracious to you; he rises to show you compassion. For the LORD is a God of justice. Blessed are all who wait for him!
Isa 54:10 Though the mountains be shaken and the hills be removed, yet my unfailing love for you will not be shaken nor my covenant of peace be removed," says the LORD, who has compassion on you.
La 3:22 Because of the LORD's great love we are not consumed, for his compassions never fail. 23 They are new every morning; great is your faithfulness.
Mic 7:18 Who is a God like you, who pardons sin and forgives the transgression of the remnant of his inheritance? You do not stay angry forever but delight to show mercy. 19 You will again have compassion on us; you will tread our sins underfoot and hurl all our iniquities into the depths of the sea.
2 Co 1:3 Praise be to the God and Father of our Lord Jesus Christ, the Father of compassion and the God of all comfort,
Jas 5:11. As you know, we consider blessed those who have persevered. You have heard of Job's perseverance and have seen what the Lord finally brought about. The Lord is full of compassion and mercy.
Mt 9:35 Jesus went through all the towns and villages, teaching in their synagogues, preaching the good news of the kingdom and healing every disease and sickness. 36 When he saw the crowds, he had compassion on them, because they were harassed and helpless, like sheep without a shepherd. 37 Then he said to his disciples, "The harvest is plentiful but the workers are few.
Mt 14:13 When Jesus heard what had happened, he withdrew by boat privately to a solitary place. Hearing of this, the crowds followed him on foot from the towns. 14 When Jesus landed and saw a large crowd, he had compassion on them and healed their sick.

Pr 14:21 He who despises his neighbor sins, but blessed is he who is kind to the needy.
Zec 7:9 "This is what the LORD Almighty says: 'Administer true justice; show mercy and compassion to one another. 10 Do not oppress the widow or the fatherless, the alien or the poor. In your hearts do not think evil of each other.'
Mt 7:12 So in everything, do to others what you would have them do to you, for this sums up the Law and the Prophets.
Lk 6:35 But love your enemies, do good to them, and lend to them without expecting to get anything back. Then your reward will be great, and you will be sons of the Most High, because he is kind to the ungrateful and wicked.
Gal 6:2 Carry each other's burdens, and in this way you will fulfill the law of Christ.
Eph 4:32 Be kind and compassionate to one another, forgiving each other, just as in Christ God forgave you.
Col 3:12 Therefore, as God's chosen people, holy and dearly loved, clothe yourselves with compassion, kindness, humility, gentleness and patience. 13 Bear with each other and forgive whatever grievances you may have against one another. Forgive as the Lord forgave you.
Mt 25:35 For I was hungry and you gave me something to eat, I was thirsty and you gave me something to drink, I was a stranger and you invited me in,
Mt 25:40 "The King will reply, 'I tell you the truth, whatever you did for one of the least of these brothers of mine, you did for me.'
Mt. 8:1 When he came down from the mountainside, large crowds followed him. 2 A man with leprosy came and knelt before him and said, "Lord, if you are willing, you can make me clean." 3 Jesus reached out his hand and touched the man. "I am willing," he said. "Be clean!" Immediately he was cured of his leprosy. 4 Then Jesus said to him, "See that you don't tell anyone. But go, show yourself to the priest and offer the gift Moses commanded, as a testimony to them."
Mt 9:27 As Jesus went on from there, two blind men followed him, calling out, "Have mercy on us, Son of David!" 28 When he had gone indoors, the blind men came to him, and he asked them, "Do you believe that I am able to do this?" "Yes, Lord," they replied. 29

Then he touched their eyes and said, "According to your faith will it be done to you"; 30 and their sight was restored. Jesus warned them sternly, "See that no one knows about this." 31 But they went out and spread the news about him all over that region.

Mk 8:22 They came to Bethsaida, and some people brought a blind man and begged Jesus to touch him. 23 He took the blind man by the hand and led him outside the village. When he had spit on the man's eyes and put his hands on him, Jesus asked, "Do you see anything?" 24 He looked up and said, "I see people; they look like trees walking around." 25 Once more Jesus put his hands on the man's eyes. Then his eyes were opened, his sight was restored, and he saw everything clearly. 26 Jesus sent him home saying, "Don't go into the village."

Chapter 5: The Bridge of Contentment Scriptures

I Tim. 6:6 But godliness with contentment is great gain. 7 For we brought nothing into the world, and we can take nothing out of it. 8 But if we have food and clothing, we will be content with that. 9 People who want to get rich fall into temptation and a trap and into many foolish and harmful desires that plunge men into ruin and destruction.

Heb 13:5 Keep your lives free from the love of money and be content with what you have, because God has said, "Never will I leave you; never will I forsake you." 6 So we say with confidence, "The Lord is my helper; I will not be afraid. What can man do to me?"

Ecc 4:8 There was a man all alone; he had neither son nor brother. There was no end to his toil; yet his eyes were not content with his wealth.

Lk 12:22 Then Jesus said to his disciples: "Therefore I tell you, do not worry about your life, what you will eat; or about your body, what you will wear. 23 Life is more than food, and the body more than clothes. 24 Consider the ravens: They do not sow or reap, they have no storeroom or barn; yet God feeds them. And how much more valuable you are than birds! 25 Who of you by worrying can add a single hour to his life? 26 Since you cannot do this very little thing, why do you worry about the rest? 27 "Consider how the lilies grow. They do not labor or spin. Yet I tell you, not even Solomon in all his splendor was dressed like one of these. 28 If that is how God clothes the grass of the field, which is here today, and tomorrow is thrown into the fire, how much more will he clothe you, O you of little faith! 29 And do not set your heart on what you will eat or drink; do not worry about it. 30 For the pagan world runs after all such things, and your Father knows that you need them. 31 But seek his kingdom, and these things will be given to you as well.

Mt. 6:25 "Therefore I tell you, do not worry about your life, what you will eat or drink; or about your body, what you will wear. Is not life more important than food, and the body more important than clothes? 26 Look at the birds of the air; they do not sow or reap or store away in barns, and yet your heavenly Father feeds them. Are you not much more valuable than they? 27 Who of you by worrying can add a single hour to his life? 28 "And why do you worry about clothes? See how the lilies of the field grow. They do not labor or spin. 29 Yet I tell you that not even Solomon in all his splendor was dressed like one of these. 30 If that is how God clothes the grass of the field, which is here today and tomorrow is thrown into the fire, will he not much more clothe you, O you of little faith? 31 So do not worry, saying, 'What shall we eat?' or 'What shall we drink?' or 'What shall we wear?' 32 For the pagans run after all these things, and your heavenly Father knows that you need them. 33 But seek first his kingdom and his righteousness, and all these things will be given to you as well.

Job 36:11 If they obey and serve him, they will spend the rest of their days in prosperity and their years in contentment. 12 But if they do not listen, they will perish by the sword and die without knowledge.

Pr. 19:23 The fear of the LORD leads to life: Then one rests content, untouched by trouble.

Isa 26:3 You will keep in perfect peace him whose mind is steadfast, because he trusts in you.

Lev. 18:4 You must obey my laws and be careful to follow my decrees. I am the LORD your God. 5 Keep my decrees and laws, for the man who obeys them will live by them. I am the LORD.

Ps 63:1 A psalm of David. When he was in the Desert of Judah. 1 O God, you are my God, earnestly I seek you; my soul thirsts for you,

my body longs for you, in a dry and weary land where there is no water. 2 I have seen you in the sanctuary and beheld your power and your glory. 3 Because your love is better than life, my lips will glorify you. 4 I will praise you as long as I live, and in your name I will lift up my hands. 5 My soul will be satisfied as with the richest of foods; with singing lips my mouth will praise you.
Nu 6:24 "The LORD bless you and keep you; 25 the LORD make his face shine upon you and be gracious to you; 26 the LORD turn his face toward you and give you peace.'"
Phil 4:11 I am not saying this because I am in need, for I have learned to be content whatever the circumstances. 12 I know what it is to be in need, and I know what it is to have plenty. I have learned the secret of being content in any and every situation, whether well fed or hungry, whether living in plenty or in want.
Nu 27:12 Then the LORD said to Moses, "Go up this mountain in the Abarim range and see the land I have given the Israelites. 13 After you have seen it, you too will be gathered to your people, as your brother Aaron was, 14 for when the community rebelled at the waters in the Desert of Zin, both of you disobeyed my command to honor me as holy before their eyes." (These were the waters of Meribah Kadesh, in the Desert of Zin.) 15 Moses said to the LORD, 16 "May the LORD, the God of the spirits of all mankind, appoint a man over this community 17 to go out and come in before them, one who will lead them out and bring them in, so the LORD's people will not be like sheep without a shepherd." 18 So the LORD said to Moses, "Take Joshua son of Nun, a man in whom is the spirit, and lay your hand on him. 19 Have him stand before Eleazar the priest and the entire assembly and commission him in their presence. 20 Give him some of your authority so the whole Israelite community will obey him. 21 He is to stand before Eleazar the priest, who will obtain decisions for him by inquiring of the Urim before the LORD. At his command he and the entire community of the Israelites will go out, and at his command they will come in." 22 Moses did as the LORD commanded him. He took Joshua and had him stand before Eleazar the priest and the whole assembly. 23 Then he laid his hands on him and commissioned him, as the LORD instructed through Moses.
Pr. 15:17 Better a meal of vegetables where there is love than a

fattened calf with hatred.
Pr.17:1 Better a dry crust with peace and quiet than a house full of feasting, with strife.
Pr.16:8 Better a little with righteousness than much gain with injustice.
Ecc. 5:18 Then I realized that it is good and proper for a man to eat and drink, and to find satisfaction in his toilsome labor under the sun during the few days of life God has given him—for this is his lot. 19 Moreover, when God gives any man wealth and possessions, and enables him to enjoy them, to accept his lot and be happy in his work—this is a gift of God. 20 He seldom reflects on the days of his life, because God keeps him occupied with gladness of heart.
2 Pe 1:3 His divine power has given us everything we need for life and godliness through our knowledge of him who called us by his own glory and goodness. 4 Through these he has given us his very great and precious promises, so that through them you may participate in the divine nature and escape the corruption in the world caused by evil desires. 5 For this very reason, make every effort to add to your faith goodness; and to goodness, knowledge; 6 and to knowledge, self-control; and to self-control, perseverance; and to perseverance, godliness; 7 and to godliness, brotherly kindness; and to brotherly kindness, love. 8 For if you possess these qualities in increasing measure, they will keep you from being ineffective and unproductive in your knowledge of our Lord Jesus Christ. 9 But if anyone does not have them, he is nearsighted and blind, and has forgotten that he has been cleansed from his past sins.

Chapter 6: The Bridge of Forgiveness Scriptures

Lk 6:36 Be merciful, just as your Father is merciful.
Eph 4:31 Get rid of all bitterness, rage and anger, brawling and slander, along with every form of malice. 32 Be kind and compassionate to one another, forgiving each other, just as in Christ God forgave you.
Mt 18:35 "This is how my heavenly Father will treat each of you unless you forgive your brother from your heart."
Mk 11:25 And when you stand praying, if you hold anything against anyone, forgive him, so that your Father in heaven may

forgive you your sins. 26 But if you do not forgive, neither will your Father who is in heaven forgive your sins.

Mt 6:14 For if you forgive men when they sin against you, your heavenly Father will also forgive you.

2 Co 2:10 If you forgive anyone, I also forgive him. And what I have forgiven—if there was anything to forgive—I have forgiven in the sight of Christ for your sake, 11 in order that Satan might not outwit us. For we are not unaware of his schemes.

Lk 17:3 So watch yourselves. "If your brother sins, rebuke him, and if he repents, forgive him.

Mt 18:21 Then Peter came to Jesus and asked, "Lord, how many times shall I forgive my brother when he sins against me? Up to seven times?" 22 Jesus answered, "I tell you, not seven times, but seventy-seven times. 23 "Therefore, the kingdom of heaven is like a king who wanted to settle accounts with his servants.

Ro 12:19 Do not take revenge, my friends, but leave room for God's wrath, for it is written: "It is mine to avenge; I will repay," says the Lord.

Pr 20:22 Do not say, "I'll pay you back for this wrong!" Wait for the LORD, and he will deliver you.

Col 1:14 in whom we have redemption, the forgiveness of sins.

Ge 33:1 Jacob looked up and there was Esau, coming with his four hundred men; so he divided the children among Leah, Rachel and the two maidservants. 2 He put the maidservants and their children in front, Leah and her children next, and Rachel and Joseph in the rear. 3 He himself went on ahead and bowed down to the ground seven times as he approached his brother. 4 But Esau ran to meet Jacob and embraced him; he threw his arms around his neck and kissed him. And they wept. 5 Then Esau looked up and saw the women and children. "Who are these with you?" he asked. Jacob answered, "They are the children God has graciously given your servant." 6 Then the maidservants and their children approached and bowed down. 7 Next, Leah and her children came and bowed down. Last of all came Joseph and Rachel, and they too bowed down. 8 Esau asked, "What do you mean by all these droves I met?" "To find favor in your eyes, my lord," he said. 9 But Esau said, "I already have plenty, my brother. Keep what you have for yourself." 10 "No, please!" said Jacob. "If I have found favor in your eyes, accept this gift from me. For to see your face is like seeing the face of God, now that you have received me favorably. 11 Please accept the present that was brought to you, for God has been gracious to me and I have all I need." And because Jacob insisted, Esau accepted it.

Php 1:12 Now I want you to know, brothers, that what has happened to me has really served to advance the gospel. 13 As a result, it has become clear throughout the whole palace guard and to everyone else that I am in chains for Christ. 14 Because of my chains, most of the brothers in the Lord have been encouraged to speak the word of God more courageously and fearlessly.

Heb 12:15 See to it that no one misses the grace of God and that no bitter root grows up to cause trouble and defile many.

Chapter 7: The Bridge of Grace Scriptures

Ro 3:21 But now a righteousness from God, apart from law, has been made known, to which the Law and the Prophets testify. 22 This righteousness from God comes through faith in Jesus Christ to all who believe. There is no difference,

Ro 4:5 However, to the man who does not work but trusts God who justifies the wicked, his faith is credited as righteousness.

2 Cor. 5:19 that God was reconciling the world to himself in Christ, not counting men's sins against them. And he has committed to us the message of reconciliation. 21 God made him who had no sin to be sin for us, so that in him we might become the righteousness of God.

I Jn 4:10 This is love: not that we loved God, but that he loved us and sent his Son as an atoning sacrifice for our sins.

Col. 2:14 having canceled the written code, with its regulations, that was against us and that stood opposed to us; he took it away, nailing it to the cross.

Ro 5:1 Therefore, since we have been justified through faith, we have peace with God through our Lord Jesus Christ, 2 through whom we have gained access by faith into this grace in which we now stand. And we rejoice in the hope of the glory of God. 3 Not only so, but we also rejoice in our sufferings, because we know that suffering produces perseverance;

Eph 3:12 In him and through faith in him we may approach God

Relationship

---

with freedom and confidence.

Ps. 36:5 Your love, O Lord, reaches to the heavens, your faithfulness to the skies.

Ps. 103: 9 He will not always accuse, nor will he harbor his anger forever; 10 he does not treat us as our sins deserve or repay us according to our iniquities. 11 For as high as the heavens are above the earth, so great is his love for those who fear him; 12 as far as the east is from the west, so far has he removed our transgressions from us. 13 As a father has compassion on his children, so the LORD has compassion on those who fear him; 14 for he knows how we are formed, he remembers that we are dust.

Ro 8:1 Therefore, there is now no condemnation for those who are in Christ Jesus,

Eph 2:13 But now in Christ Jesus you who once were far away have been brought near through the blood of Christ.

Col. 1:13 For he has rescued us from the dominion of darkness and brought us into the kingdom of the Son he loves,

Heb. 13:5 Keep your lives free from the love of money and be content with what you have, because God has said, "Never will I leave you; never will I forsake you."

Eph 2:18 For through him we both have access to the Father by one Spirit.

2 Cor 12:7 To keep me from becoming conceited because of these surpassingly great revelations, there was given me a thorn in my flesh, a messenger of Satan, to torment me. 8 Three times I pleaded with the Lord to take it away from me. 9 But he said to me, "My grace is sufficient for you, for my power is made perfect in weakness." Therefore I will boast all the more gladly about my weaknesses, so that Christ's power may rest on me.

Mt 18:21 Then Peter came to Jesus and asked, "Lord, how many times shall I forgive my brother when he sins against me? Up to seven times?" 22 Jesus answered, "I tell you, not seven times, but seventy-seven times. 23 "Therefore, the kingdom of heaven is like a king who wanted to settle accounts with his servants. 24 As he began the settlement, a man who owed him ten thousand talents was brought to him. 25 Since he was not able to pay, the master ordered that he and his wife and his children and all that he had be sold to repay the debt. 26 "The servant fell on his knees before him. 'Be patient with me,' he begged, 'and I will pay back everything.' 27 The servant's master took pity on him, canceled the debt and let him go. 28 "But when that servant went out, he found one of his fellow servants who owed him a hundred denarii. He grabbed him and began to choke him. 'Pay back what you owe me!' he demanded. 29 "His fellow servant fell to his knees and begged him, 'Be patient with me, and I will pay you back.' 30 "But he refused. Instead, he went off and had the man thrown into prison until he could pay the debt. 31 When the other servants saw what had happened, they were greatly distressed and went and told their master everything that had happened. 32 "Then the master called the servant in. 'You wicked servant,' he said, 'I canceled all that debt of yours because you begged me to. 33 Shouldn't you have had mercy on your fellow servant just as I had on you?' 34 In anger his master turned him over to the jailers to be tortured, until he should pay back all he owed. 35 "This is how my heavenly Father will treat each of you unless you forgive your brother from your heart."

Eph 4:32 Be kind and compassionate to one another, forgiving each other, just as in Christ God forgave you.

2 Tim. 2:1 You then, my son, be strong in the grace that is in Christ Jesus.

Ro 8:31 What, then, shall we say in response to this? If God is for us, who can be against us? 32 He who did not spare his own Son, but gave him up for us all—how will he not also, along with him, graciously give us all things? 33 Who will bring any charge against those whom God has chosen? It is God who justifies. 34 Who is he that condemns? Christ Jesus, who died—more than that, who was raised to life—is at the right hand of God and is also interceding for us. 35 Who shall separate us from the love of Christ? Shall trouble or hardship or persecution or famine or nakedness or danger or sword? 36 As it is written: "For your sake we face death all day long; we are considered as sheep to be slaughtered." 37 No, in all these things we are more than conquerors through him who loved us. 38 For I am convinced that neither death nor life, neither angels nor demons, neither the present nor the future, nor any powers, 39 neither height nor depth, nor anything else in all creation, will be able to separate us from the love of God that is in Christ Jesus our Lord.

Chapter 8: The Bridge of Hope Scriptures

Ps 119:81 My soul faints with longing for your salvation, but I have put my hope in your word.
Ps 119:114 You are my refuge and my shield; I have put my hope in your word.
Ps 119:116 Sustain me according to your promise, and I will live; do not let my hopes be dashed.
Ro 5:1 Therefore, since we have been justified through faith, we have peace with God through our Lord Jesus Christ, 2 through whom we have gained access by faith into this grace in which we now stand. And we rejoice in the hope of the glory of God.
Ro 8:23 Not only so, but we ourselves, who have the first fruits of the Spirit, groan inwardly as we wait eagerly for our adoption as sons, the redemption of our bodies.
Tit 2:11 For the grace of God that brings salvation has appeared to all men. 12 It teaches us to say "No" to ungodliness and worldly passions, and to live self-controlled, upright and godly lives in this present age, 13 while we wait for the blessed hope—the glorious appearing of our great God and Savior, Jesus Christ,
Tit 3:4 But when the kindness and love of God our Savior appeared, 5 he saved us, not because of righteous things we had done, but because of his mercy. He saved us through the washing of rebirth and renewal by the Holy Spirit, 6 whom he poured out on us generously through Jesus Christ our Savior, 7 so that, having been justified by his grace, we might become heirs having the hope of eternal life.
I Pe 1:13 Therefore, prepare your minds for action; be self-controlled; set your hope fully on the grace to be given you when Jesus Christ is revealed.
1 Jn 3:2 Dear friends, now we are children of God, and what we will be has not yet been made known. But we know that when he appears, we shall be like him, for we shall see him as he is. 3 Everyone who has this hope in him purifies himself, just as he is pure.
Ps 43:5 Why are you downcast, O my soul? Why so disturbed within me? Put your hope in God, for I will yet praise him, my Savior and my God.

Ps 62:5 Find rest, O my soul, in God alone; my hope comes from him. 6 He alone is my rock and my salvation; he is my fortress, I will not be shaken.

Ps 130:7 O Israel, put your hope in the LORD, for with the LORD is unfailing love and with him is full redemption.

Ps 146:5 Blessed is he whose help is the God of Jacob, whose hope is in the LORD his God, 6 the Maker of heaven and earth, the sea, and everything in them— the LORD, who remains faithful forever.

Hab 3:17 Though the fig tree does not bud and there are no grapes on the vines, though the olive crop fails and the fields produce no food, though there are no sheep in the pen and no cattle in the stalls, 18 yet I will rejoice in the LORD, I will be joyful in God my Savior. 19 The Sovereign LORD is my strength; he makes my feet like the feet of a deer, he enables me to go on the heights. For the director of music. On my stringed instruments.

1 Ti 4:10 (and for this we labor and strive), that we have put our hope in the living God, who is the Savior of all men, and especially of those who believe.

Ps 16:8 I have set the LORD always before me. Because he is at my right hand, I will not be shaken. 9 Therefore my heart is glad and my tongue rejoices; my body also will rest secure, 10 because you will not abandon me to the grave, nor will you let your Holy One see decay. 11 You have made known to me the path of life; you will fill me with joy in your presence, with eternal pleasures at your right hand.

Ps 25:3 No one whose hope is in you will ever be put to shame, but they will be put to shame who are treacherous without excuse.

Ps 25:21 May integrity and uprightness protect me, because my hope is in you.

Ps 33:18 But the eyes of the LORD are on those who fear him, on those whose hope is in his unfailing love, 19 to deliver them from death and keep them alive in famine. 20 We wait in hope for the LORD; he is our help and our shield. 21 In him our hearts rejoice, for we trust in his holy name. 22 May your unfailing love rest upon us, O LORD, even as we put our hope in you.

Ps 119:116 Sustain me according to your promise, and I will live; do not let my hopes be dashed.

Ps 146:5 Blessed is he whose help is the God of Jacob, whose hope is in the LORD his God, 6 the Maker of heaven and earth, the sea, and everything in them— the LORD, who remains faithful forever. 7 He upholds the cause of the oppressed and gives food to the hungry. The LORD sets prisoners free, 8 the LORD gives sight to the blind, the LORD lifts up those who are bowed down, the LORD loves the righteous. 9 The LORD watches over the alien and sustains the fatherless and the widow, but he frustrates the ways of the wicked.

Isa 30:18 Yet the LORD longs to be gracious to you; he rises to show you compassion. For the LORD is a God of justice. Blessed are all who wait for him!

Isa 40:31 but those who hope in the LORD will renew their strength. They will soar on wings like eagles; they will run and not grow weary, they will walk and not be faint.

Jer 17:7 "But blessed is the man who trusts in the LORD, whose confidence is in him. 8 He will be like a tree planted by the water that sends out its roots by the stream. It does not fear when heat comes; its leaves are always green. It has no worries in a year of drought and never fails to bear fruit."

La 3:21 Yet this I call to mind and therefore I have hope: 22 Because of the LORD's great love we are not consumed, for his compassions never fail.

Mic 7:7 But as for me, I watch in hope for the LORD, I wait for God my Savior; my God will hear me. 8 Do not gloat over me, my enemy! Though I have fallen, I will rise. Though I sit in darkness, the LORD will be my light.

Ro 5:5 And hope does not disappoint us, because God has poured out his love into our hearts by the Holy Spirit, whom he has given us.

Ro 15:13 May the God of hope fill you with all joy and peace as you trust in him, so that you may overflow with hope by the power of the Holy Spirit.

Eph 1:18 I pray also that the eyes of your heart may be enlightened in order that you may know the hope to which he has called you, the riches of his glorious inheritance in the saints,

1 Pe 1:3 Praise be to the God and Father of our Lord Jesus Christ! In his great mercy he has given us new birth into a living hope through the resurrection of Jesus Christ from the dead,

Heb 11:1 Now faith is being sure of what we hope for and certain of what we do not see.

1 Pe 3:15 But in your hearts set apart Christ as Lord. Always be prepared to give an answer to everyone who asks you to give the reason for the hope that you have. But do this with gentleness and respect,

1 Jn 3:2 Dear friends, now we are children of God, and what we will be has not yet been made known. But we know that when he appears, we shall be like him, for we shall see him as he is. 3 Everyone who has this hope in him purifies himself, just as he is pure.

Chapter 9: The Bridge of Hospitality Scriptures

1 Pe 4:9 Offer hospitality to one another without grumbling.

Dt 15:11 There will always be poor people in the land. Therefore I command you to be openhanded toward your brothers and toward the poor and needy in your land.

Mt 10:42 And if anyone gives even a cup of cold water to one of these little ones because he is my disciple, I tell you the truth, he will certainly not lose his reward."

1 Pe 4:11 If anyone speaks, he should do it as one speaking the very words of God. If anyone serves, he should do it with the strength God provides, so that in all things God may be praised through Jesus Christ. To him be the glory and the power for ever and ever. Amen.

Heb. 13:2 Do not forget to entertain strangers, for by so doing some people have entertained angels without knowing it.

Is. 58:7 Is it not to share your food with the hungry and to provide the poor wanderer with shelter— when you see the naked, to clothe him, and not to turn away from your own flesh and blood?

Lk 14:13 But when you give a banquet, invite the poor, the crippled, the lame, the blind,

2 Ki 6:22 "Do not kill them," he answered. "Would you kill men you have captured with your own sword or bow? Set food and water before them so that they may eat and drink and then go back to their master." 23 So he prepared a great feast for them, and after they had finished eating and drinking, he sent them away, and they returned to their master. So the bands from Aram stopped raiding

Relationship

Israel's territory.

Ro 12:20 On the contrary: "If your enemy is hungry, feed him; if he is thirsty, give him something to drink. In doing this, you will heap burning coals on his head."

1 Jn 3:17 If anyone has material possessions and sees his brother in need but has no pity on him, how can the love of God be in him?

Ac 20:35 In everything I did, I showed you that by this kind of hard work we must help the weak, remembering the words the Lord Jesus himself said: 'It is more blessed to give than to receive.'"

1 Ki 17:10 So he went to Zarephath. When he came to the town gate, a widow was there gathering sticks. He called to her and asked, "Would you bring me a little water in a jar so I may have a drink?" 11 As she was going to get it, he called, "And bring me, please, a piece of bread." 12 "As surely as the LORD your God lives," she replied, "I don't have any bread—only a handful of flour in a jar and a little oil in a jug. I am gathering a few sticks to take home and make a meal for myself and my son, that we may eat it—and die." 13 Elijah said to her, "Don't be afraid. Go home and do as you have said. But first make a small cake of bread for me from what you have and bring it to me, and then make something for yourself and your son. 14 For this is what the LORD, the God of Israel, says: 'The jar of flour will not be used up and the jug of oil will not run dry until the day the LORD gives rain on the land.'" 15 She went away and did as Elijah had told her. So there was food every day for Elijah and for the woman and her family. 16 For the jar of flour was not used up and the jug of oil did not run dry, in keeping with the word of the LORD spoken by Elijah.

2 Ki 4:8 One day Elisha went to Shunem. And a well-to-do woman was there, who urged him to stay for a meal. So whenever he came by, he stopped there to eat. 9 She said to her husband, "I know that this man who often comes our way is a holy man of God. 10 Let's make a small room on the roof and put in it a bed and a table, a chair and a lamp for him. Then he can stay there whenever he comes to us." 11 One day when Elisha came, he went up to his room and lay down there.

Ac 12:11 Then Peter came to himself and said, "Now I know without a doubt that the Lord sent his angel and rescued me from Herod's clutches and from everything the Jewish people were anticipating." 12 When this had dawned on him, he went to the house of Mary the mother of John, also called Mark, where many people had gathered and were praying. 13 Peter knocked at the outer entrance, and a servant girl named Rhoda came to answer the door. 14 When she recognized Peter's voice, she was so overjoyed she ran back without opening it and exclaimed, "Peter is at the door!" 15 "You're out of your mind," they told her. When she kept insisting that it was so, they said, "It must be his angel." 16 But Peter kept on knocking, and when they opened the door and saw him, they were astonished. 17 Peter motioned with his hand for them to be quiet and described how the Lord had brought him out of prison. "Tell James and the brothers about this," he said, and then he left for another place.

Ac 16:13 On the Sabbath we went outside the city gate to the river, where we expected to find a place of prayer. We sat down and began to speak to the women who had gathered there. 14 One of those listening was a woman named Lydia, a dealer in purple cloth from the city of Thyatira, who was a worshiper of God. The Lord opened her heart to respond to Paul's message. 15 When she and the members of her household were baptized, she invited us to her home. "If you consider me a believer in the Lord," she said, "come and stay at my house." And she persuaded us.

Ac 16:40 After Paul and Silas came out of the prison, they went to Lydia's house, where they met with the brothers and encouraged them. Then they left.

1 Co 16:19 The churches in the province of Asia send you greetings. Aquila and Priscilla greet you warmly in the Lord, and so does the church that meets at their house.

Mt 25:35 For I was hungry and you gave me something to eat, I was thirsty and you gave me something to drink, I was a stranger and you invited me in, 36 I needed clothes and you clothed me, I was sick and you looked after me, I was in prison and you came to visit me.'

Mt 25:40 "The King will reply, 'I tell you the truth, whatever you did for one of the least of these brothers of mine, you did for me.'

Lev 23:22 " 'When you reap the harvest of your land, do not reap to the very edges of your field or gather the gleanings of your harvest. Leave them for the poor and the alien. I am the LORD your God.' "

Isa 58:6 "Is not this the kind of fasting I have chosen: to loose the chains of injustice and untie the cords of the yoke, to set the oppressed free and break every yoke? 7 Is it not to share your food with the hungry and to provide the poor wanderer with shelter—when you see the naked, to clothe him, and not to turn away from your own flesh and blood? 8 Then your light will break forth like the dawn, and your healing will quickly appear; then your righteousness will go before you, and the glory of the LORD will be your rear guard. 9 Then you will call, and the LORD will answer; you will cry for help, and he will say: Here am I. "If you do away with the yoke of oppression, with the pointing finger and malicious talk,

Lk 14:12 Then Jesus said to his host, "When you give a luncheon or dinner, do not invite your friends, your brothers or relatives, or your rich neighbors; if you do, they may invite you back and so you will be repaid. 13 But when you give a banquet, invite the poor, the crippled, the lame, the blind, 14 and you will be blessed. Although they cannot repay you, you will be repaid at the resurrection of the righteous."

Ac 5:42 Day after day, in the temple courts and from house to house, they never stopped teaching and proclaiming the good news that Jesus is the Christ.

Mt 10:9 Do not take along any gold or silver or copper in your belts; 10 take no bag for the journey, or extra tunic, or sandals or a staff; for the worker is worth his keep. 11 "Whatever town or village you enter, search for some worthy person there and stay at his house until you leave.

Chapter 10: The Bridge of Impartiality Scriptures

Lev 19:15 Do not pervert justice; do not show partiality to the poor or favoritism to the great, but judge your neighbor fairly.

Dt 1:17 Do not show partiality in judging; hear both small and great alike. Do not be afraid of any man, for judgment belongs to God. Bring me any case too hard for you, and I will hear it.

Dt 10:17 For the LORD your God is God of gods and Lord of lords, the great God, mighty and awesome, who shows no partiality and accepts no bribes.

Ro 2:11 For God does not show favoritism.

Pr 28:21 To show partiality is not good— yet a man will do wrong for a piece of bread.

Mt 22:16 They sent their disciples to him along with the Herodians. "Teacher," they said, "we know you are a man of integrity and that you teach the way of God in accordance with the truth. You aren't swayed by men, because you pay no attention to who they are.

Jas 2:9 But if you show favoritism, you sin and are convicted by the law as lawbreakers.

Lk 10:29 But he wanted to justify himself, so he asked Jesus, "And who is my neighbor?"
30 In reply Jesus said: "A man was going down from Jerusalem to Jericho, when he fell into the hands of robbers. They stripped him of his clothes, beat him and went away, leaving him half dead. 31 A priest happened to be going down the same road, and when he saw the man, he passed by on the other side. 32 So too, a Levite, when he came to the place and saw him, passed by on the other side. 33 But a Samaritan, as he traveled, came where the man was; and when he saw him, he took pity on him. 34 He went to him and bandaged his wounds, pouring on oil and wine. Then he put the man on his own donkey, took him to an inn and took
care of him. 35 The next day he took out two silver coins and gave them to the innkeeper. 'Look after him,' he said, 'and when I return, I will reimburse you for any extra expense you may have.' 36 "Which of these three do you think was a neighbor to the man who fell into the hands of robbers?" 37 The expert in the law replied, "The one who had mercy on him." Jesus told him, "Go and do likewise."

Jas 2:1 My brothers, as believers in our glorious Lord Jesus Christ, don't show favoritism. 2 Suppose a man comes into your meeting wearing a gold ring and fine clothes, and a poor man in shabby clothes also comes in. 3 If you show special attention to the man wearing fine clothes and say, "Here's a good seat for you," but say to the poor man, "You stand there" or "Sit on the floor by my feet," 4 have you not discriminated among yourselves and become judges with evil thoughts? 5 Listen, my dear brothers: Has not God chosen those who are poor in the eyes of the world to be rich in faith and to inherit the kingdom he promised those who love him? 6 But you have insulted the poor. Is it not the rich who are exploiting you? Are they not the ones who are dragging you into court? 7 Are they not the ones who are slandering the noble name of him to whom you belong? 8 If you really keep the royal law found in Scripture, "Love your neighbor as yourself," you are doing right. 9 But if you show favoritism, you sin and are convicted by the law as lawbreakers. 10 For whoever keeps the whole law and yet stumbles at just one point is guilty of breaking all of it. 11 For he who said, "Do not commit adultery," also said, "Do not murder." If you do not commit adultery but do commit murder, you have become a lawbreaker. 12 Speak and act as those who are going to be judged by the law that gives freedom,

Mk 7: 21 For from within, out of men's hearts, come evil thoughts, sexual immorality, theft, murder, adultery, 22 greed, malice, deceit, lewdness, envy, slander, arrogance and folly. 23 All these evils come from inside and make a man 'unclean.'"

Chapter 11: The Bridge of Integrity Scriptures

I Ch 29:17 I know, my God, that you test the heart and are pleased with integrity. All these things have I given willingly and with honest intent. And now I have seen with joy how willingly your people who are here have given to you.

Ps. 25:21 May integrity and uprightness protect me, because my hope is in you.

Ps. 41:12 In my integrity you uphold me and set me in your presence forever.

Ps 84:11 For the LORD God is a sun and shield; the LORD bestows favor and honor; no good thing does he withhold from those whose walk is blameless.

Ps 112:4 Even in darkness light dawns for the upright, for the gracious and compassionate and righteous man.

Pr 2:7 He holds victory in store for the upright, he is a shield to those whose walk is blameless, 8 for he guards the course of the just and protects the way of his faithful ones.

Isa 57:2 Those who walk uprightly enter into peace; they find rest as they lie in death.

I Ki 9:4 "As for you, if you walk before me in integrity of heart and uprightness, as David your father did, and do all I command and

Scriptures

observe my decrees and laws, 5 I will establish your royal throne over Israel forever, as I promised David your father when I said, 'You shall never fail to have a man on the throne of Israel.'

Pr. 10:9 The man of integrity walks securely, but he who takes crooked paths will be found out.

Pr 11:3 The integrity of the upright guides them, but the unfaithful are destroyed by their duplicity.

Pr 13:6 Righteousness guards the man of integrity, but wickedness overthrows the sinner.

Lk 16:10 "Whoever can be trusted with very little can also be trusted with much, and whoever is dishonest with very little will also be dishonest with much.

Mt 16:26 What good will it be for a man if he gains the whole world, yet forfeits his soul? Or what can a man give in exchange for his soul?

Heb 11:32 And what more shall I say? I do not have time to tell about Gideon, Barak, Samson, Jephthah, David, Samuel and the prophets, 33 who through faith conquered kingdoms, administered justice, and gained what was promised; who shut the mouths of lions, 34 quenched the fury of the flames, and escaped the edge of the sword; whose weakness was turned to strength; and who became powerful in battle and routed foreign armies. 35 Women received back their dead, raised to life again. Others were tortured and refused to be released, so that they might gain a better resurrection. 36 Some faced jeers and flogging, while still others were chained and put in prison. 37 They were stoned ; they were sawed in two; they were put to death by the sword. They went about in sheepskins and goatskins, destitute, persecuted and mistreated— 38 the world was not worthy of them. They wandered in deserts and mountains, and in caves and holes in the ground. 39 These were all commended for their faith, yet none of them received what had been promised.

Gal 5:16 So I say, live by the Spirit, and you will not gratify the desires of the sinful nature.

Ps 37:7 Be still before the LORD and wait patiently for him; do not fret when men succeed in their ways, when they carry out their wicked schemes. 8 Refrain from anger and turn from wrath; do not fret—it leads only to evil. 9 For evil men will be cut off, but those

who hope in the LORD will inherit the land.
Mt 6:19 "Do not store up for yourselves treasures on earth, where moth and rust destroy, and where thieves break in and steal. 20 But store up for yourselves treasures in heaven, where moth and rust do not destroy, and where thieves do not break in and steal. 21 For where your treasure is, there your heart will be also.
Ro 12:3 For by the grace given me I say to every one of you: Do not think of yourself more highly than you ought, but rather think of yourself with sober judgment, in accordance with the measure of faith God has given you.
1 Tim 6:17 Command those who are rich in this present world not to be arrogant nor to put their hope in wealth, which is so uncertain, but to put their hope in God, who richly provides us with everything for our enjoyment. 18 Command them to do good, to be rich in good deeds, and to be generous and willing to share. 19 In this way they will lay up treasure for themselves as a firm foundation for the coming age, so that they may take hold of the life that is truly life.
Tit 2:6 Similarly, encourage the young men to be self-controlled. 7 In everything set them an example by doing what is good. In your teaching show integrity, seriousness 8 and soundness of speech that cannot be condemned, so that those who oppose you may be ashamed because they have nothing bad to say about us.

Chapter 12: The Bridge of Intimacy Scriptures

Ps 139 1 O LORD, you have searched me and you know me. 2 You know when I sit and when I rise; you perceive my thoughts from afar. 3 You discern my going out and my lying down; you are familiar with all my ways. 4 Before a word is on my tongue you know it completely, O LORD. 5 You hem me in—behind and before; you have laid your hand upon me. 6 Such knowledge is too wonderful for me, too lofty for me to attain. 7 Where can I go from your Spirit? Where can I flee from your presence? 8 If I go up to the heavens, you are there; if I make my bed in the depths, you are there. 9 If I rise on the wings of the dawn, if I settle on the far side of the sea, 10 even there your hand will guide me, your right hand will hold me fast. 11 If I say, "Surely the darkness will hide me and the light become night around me," 12 even the darkness will not be dark to you; the night will shine like the day, for darkness is as light to you. 13 For you created my inmost being; you knit me together in my mother's womb. 14 I praise you because I am fearfully and wonderfully made; your works are wonderful, I know that full well. 15 My frame was not hidden from you when I was made in the secret place. When I was woven together in the depths of the earth, 16 your eyes saw my unformed body. All the days ordained for me were written in your book before one of them came to be. 17 How precious to me are your thoughts, O God! How vast is the sum of them! 18 Were I to count them, they would outnumber the grains of sand. When I awake, I am still with you. 19 If only you would slay the wicked, O God! Away from me, you bloodthirsty men! 20 They speak of you with evil intent; your adversaries misuse your name. 21 Do I not hate those who hate you, O LORD, and abhor those who rise up against you? 22 I have nothing but hatred for them; I count them my enemies. 23 Search me, O God, and know my heart; test me and know my anxious thoughts. 24 See if there is any offensive way in me, and lead me in the way everlasting.

Jn 15:1 "I am the true vine, and my Father is the gardener. 2 He cuts off every branch in me that bears no fruit, while every branch that does bear fruit he prunes so that it will be even more fruitful. 3 You are already clean because of the word I have spoken to you. 4 Remain in me, and I will remain in you. No branch can bear fruit by itself; it must remain in the vine. Neither can you bear fruit unless you remain in me. 5 "I am the vine; you are the branches. If a man remains in me and I in him, he will bear much fruit; apart from me you can do nothing. 6 If anyone does not remain in me, he is like a branch that is thrown away and withers; such branches are picked up, thrown into the fire and burned. 7 If you remain in me and my words remain in you, ask whatever you wish, and it will be given you. 8 This is to my Father's glory, that you bear much fruit, showing yourselves to be my disciples. 9 "As the Father has loved me, so have I loved you. Now remain in my love. 10 If you obey my commands, you will remain in my love, just as I have obeyed my Father's commands and remain in his love. 11 I have told you this so that my joy may be in you and that your joy may be complete. 12 My command is this: Love each other as I have loved you. 13 Greater love has no one than this, that he lay down his life for his

friends. 14 You are my friends if you do what I command. 15 I no longer call you servants, because a servant does not know his master's business. Instead, I have called you friends, for everything that I learned from my Father I have made known to you.
Eph 3:16 I pray that out of his glorious riches he may strengthen you with power through his Spirit in your inner being, 17 so that Christ may dwell in your hearts through faith. And I pray that you, being rooted and established in love, 18 may have power, together with all the saints, to grasp how wide and long and high and deep is the love of Christ, 19 and to know this love that surpasses knowledge—that you may be filled to the measure of all the fullness of God.
Php 2:5 Your attitude should be the same as that of Christ Jesus
Php 4:8 Finally, brothers, whatever is true, whatever is noble, whatever is right, whatever is pure, whatever is lovely, whatever is admirable—if anything is excellent or praiseworthy—think about such things.
2 Co 10:5 We demolish arguments and every pretension that sets itself up against the knowledge of God, and we take captive every thought to make it obedient to Christ.

Chapter 13: The Bridge of "Love" Scriptures

Ps 91:14 "Because he loves me," says the LORD, "I will rescue him; I will protect him, for he acknowledges my name.
Jn 14:31 but the world must learn that I love the Father and that I do exactly what my Father has commanded me. "Come now; let us leave.
Jn 15:9 "As the Father has loved me, so have I loved you. Now remain in my love.
Eph 5:24 Now as the church submits to Christ, so also wives should submit to their husbands in everything.
Pr 8:17 I love those who love me, and those who seek me find me.
Jn 14:21 Whoever has my commands and obeys them, he is the one who loves me. He who loves me will be loved by my Father, and I too will love him and show myself to him."
Lk 19:10 For the Son of Man came to seek and to save what was lost."

Lk 23:34 Jesus said, "Father, forgive them, for they do not know what they are doing." And they divided up his clothes by casting lots.

Gal 2:20 I have been crucified with Christ and I no longer live, but Christ lives in me. The life I live in the body, I live by faith in the Son of God, who loved me and gave himself for me.

Jn 15:13 Greater love has no one than this, that he lay down his life for his friends.

1 Jn 3:16 This is how we know what love is: Jesus Christ laid down his life for us. And we ought to lay down our lives for our brothers.

Rev 1:5 and from Jesus Christ, who is the faithful witness, the firstborn from the dead, and the ruler of the kings of the earth. To him who loves us and has freed us from our sins by his blood

Heb 7:25 Therefore he is able to save completely those who come to God through him, because he always lives to intercede for them.

Heb 9:24 For Christ did not enter a man-made sanctuary that was only a copy of the true one; he entered heaven itself, now to appear for us in God's presence.

Ps 68:18 When you ascended on high, you led captives in your train; you received gifts from men, even from the rebellious— that you, O LORD God, might dwell there.

Jn 16:7 But I tell you the truth: It is for your good that I am going away. Unless I go away, the Counselor will not come to you; but if I go, I will send him to you.

Rev 3:19 Those whom I love I rebuke and discipline. So be earnest, and repent.

SS 8:7 Many waters cannot quench love; rivers cannot wash it away. If one were to give all the wealth of his house for love, it would be utterly scorned.

2 Co 5:14 For Christ's love compels us, because we are convinced that one died for all, and therefore all died.

Jn 13:1 It was just before the Passover Feast. Jesus knew that the time had come for him to leave this world and go to the Father. Having loved his own who were in the world, he now showed them the full extent of his love.

Ro 8:35 Who shall separate us from the love of Christ? Shall trouble or hardship or persecution or famine or nakedness or danger or sword?

Relationship

---

1 Jn 4:7 Dear friends, let us love one another, for love comes from God. Everyone who loves has been born of God and knows God.
1 Jn 4:21 And he has given us this command: Whoever loves God must also love his brother.
Jn 13:34 "A new command I give you: Love one another. As I have loved you, so you must love one another.
Jn 15:12 My command is this: Love each other as I have loved you.
1 Jn 3:23 And this is his command: to believe in the name of his Son, Jesus Christ, and to love one another as he commanded us.
Eph 5:2 and live a life of love, just as Christ loved us and gave himself up for us as a fragrant offering and sacrifice to God.
Ga 5:22 But the fruit of the Spirit is love, joy, peace, patience, kindness, goodness, faithfulness,
Col 1:8 And he is the head of the body, the church; he is the beginning and the firstborn from among the dead, so that in everything he might have the supremacy.
1 Pe 1:22 Now that you have purified yourselves by obeying the truth so that you have sincere love for your brothers, love one another deeply, from the heart.
1 Co 13:4 Love is patient, love is kind. It does not envy, it does not boast, it is not proud. 5 It is not rude, it is not self-seeking, it is not easily angered, it keeps no record of wrongs. 6 Love does not delight in evil but rejoices with the truth. 7 It always protects, always trusts, always hopes, always perseveres.
1 Th 1:3 We continually remember before our God and Father your work produced by faith, your labor prompted by love, and your endurance inspired by hope in our Lord Jesus Christ
Heb 6:10 God is not unjust; he will not forget your work and the love you have shown him as you have helped his people and continue to help them.
1 Co 13:8 Love never fails. But where there are prophecies, they will cease; where there are tongues, they will be stilled; where there is knowledge, it will pass away.
1 Co 13:13 And now these three remain: faith, hope and love. But the greatest of these is love.
Mt 22:37 Jesus replied: " 'Love the Lord your God with all your heart and with all your soul and with all your mind.' 38 This is the first and greatest commandment. 39 And the second is like it: 'Love

your neighbor as yourself.'
1 Co 13:1 If I speak in the tongues of men and of angels, but have not love, I am only a resounding gong or a clanging cymbal. 2 If I have the gift of prophecy and can fathom all mysteries and all knowledge, and if I have a faith that can move mountains, but have not love, I am nothing.
Php 1:9 And this is my prayer: that your love may abound more and more in knowledge and depth of insight
1 Th 3:12 May the Lord make your love increase and overflow for each other and for everyone else, just as ours does for you.
Ro 12:9 Love must be sincere. Hate what is evil; cling to what is good.
2 Co 6:6 in purity, understanding, patience and kindness; in the Holy Spirit and in sincere love;
2 Co 8:8 I am not commanding you, but I want to test the sincerity of your love by comparing it with the earnestness of others.
1 Jn 3:18 Dear children, let us not love with words or tongue but with actions and in truth.
1 Pe 1:22 Now that you have purified yourselves by obeying the truth so that you have sincere love for your brothers, love one another deeply, from the heart.
Ga 6:10 Therefore, as we have opportunity, let us do good to all people, especially to those who belong to the family of believers.
Mt Ch. 25 (Refer to your own Bible.)
Eph 4:32 Be kind and compassionate to one another, forgiving each other, just as in Christ God forgave you.

Chapter 14: The Bridge of Prayer Scriptures

Neh 9 (Refer to your own Bible.)
Jer 29:12 Then you will call upon me and come and pray to me, and I will listen to you.
Jer 33:3 'Call to me and I will answer you and tell you great and unsearchable things you do not know.'
Mt 26:41 "Watch and pray so that you will not fall into temptation. The spirit is willing, but the body is weak."
Heb 4:16 Let us then approach the throne of grace with confidence, so that we may receive mercy and find grace to help us in our time

of need.

Jas 5:13 Is any one of you in trouble? He should pray. Is anyone happy? Let him sing songs of praise. 14 Is any one of you sick? He should call the elders of the church to pray over him and anoint him with oil in the name of the Lord. 15 And the prayer offered in faith will make the sick person well; the Lord will raise him up. If he has sinned, he will be forgiven. 16 Therefore confess your sins to each other and pray for each other so that you may be healed. The prayer of a righteous man is powerful and effective.

Eph 6:18 And pray in the Spirit on all occasions with all kinds of prayers and requests. With this in mind, be alert and always keep on praying for all the saints.

I Th 5:17 pray continually;

Dt. 4:7 What other nation is so great as to have their gods near them the way the LORD our God is near us whenever we pray to him?

2 Ch 7:14 if my people, who are called by my name, will humble themselves and pray and seek my face and turn from their wicked ways, then will I hear from heaven and will forgive their sin and will heal their land.

Isa. 30:19 O people of Zion, who live in Jerusalem, you will weep no more. How gracious he will be when you cry for help! As soon as he hears, he will answer you.

Jas 5:15 And the prayer offered in faith will make the sick person well; the Lord will raise him up. If he has sinned, he will be forgiven.

Ps. 38:10 My heart pounds, my strength fails me; even the light has gone from my eyes.

Ps 46:10 "Be still, and know that I am God; I will be exalted among the nations, I will be exalted in the earth."

Mt 6:5 "And when you pray, do not be like the hypocrites, for they love to pray standing in the synagogues and on the street corners to be seen by men. I tell you the truth, they have received their reward in full. 6 But when you pray, go into your room, close the door and pray to your Father, who is unseen. Then your Father, who sees what is done in secret, will reward you. 7 And when you pray, do not keep on babbling like pagans, for they think they will be heard because of their many words. 8 Do not be like them, for your Father knows what you need before you ask him.

Mk 11:25 And when you stand praying, if you hold anything against anyone, forgive him, so that your Father in heaven may forgive you your sins."
Col 4:2 Devote yourselves to prayer, being watchful and thankful.
Job 22:27 You will pray to him, and he will hear you, and you will fulfill your vows.
Isa 65:24 Before they call I will answer; while they are still speaking I will hear.
Mt 7:7 "Ask and it will be given to you; seek and you will find; knock and the door will be opened to you. 8 For everyone who asks receives; he who seeks finds; and to him who knocks, the door will be opened.
Mt 21:22 If you believe, you will receive whatever you ask for in prayer."
Mk 11:24 Therefore I tell you, whatever you ask for in prayer, believe that you have received it, and it will be yours.
Jn 14:13 And I will do whatever you ask in my name, so that the Son may bring glory to the Father. 14 You may ask me for anything in my name, and I will do it.
Jn 16: 23 In that day you will no longer ask me anything. I tell you the truth, my Father will give you whatever you ask in my name. 24 Until now you have not asked for anything in my name. Ask and you will receive, and your joy will be complete.
I Pe 3:12 For the eyes of the Lord are on the righteous and his ears are attentive to their prayer, but the face of the Lord is against those who do evil."
I Jn 3:21 Dear friends, if our hearts do not condemn us, we have confidence before God 22 and receive from him anything we ask, because we obey his commands and do what pleases him.
I Jn 5:14 This is the confidence we have in approaching God: that if we ask anything according to his will, he hears us. 15 And if we know that he hears us—whatever we ask—we know that we have what we asked of him.
Rom 8:26 In the same way, the Spirit helps us in our weakness. We do not know what we ought to pray for, but the Spirit himself intercedes for us with groans that words cannot express. 27 And he who searches our hearts knows the mind of the Spirit, because the Spirit intercedes for the saints in accordance with God's will.

Relationship

Chapter 15: The Bridge of Transparency Scriptures

Mt 8:20 Jesus replied, "Foxes have holes and birds of the air have nests, but the Son of Man has no place to lay his head."
Mt 9:2 Some men brought to him a paralytic, lying on a mat. When Jesus saw their faith, he said to the paralytic, "Take heart, son; your sins are forgiven." 3 At this, some of the teachers of the law said to themselves, "This fellow is blaspheming!" 4 Knowing their thoughts, Jesus said, "Why do you entertain evil thoughts in your hearts? 5 Which is easier to say, 'Your sins are forgiven,' or to say, 'Get up and walk'? 6 But so that you may know that the Son of Man has authority on earth to forgive sins...." Then he said to the paralytic, "Get up, take your mat and go home." 7 And the man got up and went home. 8 When the crowd saw this, they were filled with awe; and they praised God, who had given such authority to men.
Mt 12:25 Jesus knew their thoughts and said to them, "Every kingdom divided against itself will be ruined, and every city or household divided against itself will not stand. 26 If Satan drives out Satan, he is divided against himself. How then can his kingdom stand? 27 And if I drive out demons by Beelzebub, by whom do your people drive them out? So then, they will be your judges. 28 But if I drive out demons by the Spirit of God, then the kingdom of God has come upon you. 29 "Or again, how can anyone enter a strong man's house and carry off his possessions unless he first ties up the strong man? Then he can rob his house.
Mt 12:46 While Jesus was still talking to the crowd, his mother and brothers stood outside, wanting to speak to him. 47 Someone told him, "Your mother and brothers are standing outside, wanting to speak to you." 48 He replied to him, "Who is my mother, and who are my brothers?" 49 Pointing to his disciples, he said, "Here are my mother and my brothers. 50 For whoever does the will of my Father in heaven is my brother and sister and mother."
Mt 13:54 Coming to his hometown, he began teaching the people in their synagogue, and they were amazed. "Where did this man get this wisdom and these miraculous powers?" they asked. 55 "Isn't this the carpenter's son? Isn't his mother's name Mary, and aren't his brothers James, Joseph, Simon and Judas? 56 Aren't all his

sisters with us? Where then did this man get all these things?" 57 And they took offense at him. But Jesus said to them, "Only in his hometown and in his own house is a prophet without honor." 58 And he did not do many miracles there because of their lack of faith.

Mt 16:21 From that time on Jesus began to explain to his disciples that he must go to Jerusalem and suffer many things at the hands of the elders, chief priests and teachers of the law, and that he must be killed and on the third day be raised to life. 22 Peter took him aside and began to rebuke him. "Never, Lord!" he said. "This shall never happen to you!" 23 Jesus turned and said to Peter, "Get behind me, Satan! You are a stumbling block to me; you do not have in mind the things of God, but the things of men." 24 Then Jesus said to his disciples, "If anyone would come after me, he must deny himself and take up his cross and follow me. 25 For whoever wants to save his life will lose it, but whoever loses his life for me will find it. 26 What good will it be for a man if he gains the whole world, yet forfeits his soul? Or what can a man give in exchange for his soul? 27 For the Son of Man is going to come in his Father's glory with his angels, and then he will reward each person according to what he has done. 28 I tell you the truth, some who are standing here will not taste death before they see the Son of Man coming in his kingdom."

Mt 17:1 After six days Jesus took with him Peter, James and John the brother of James, and led them up a high mountain by themselves. 2 There he was transfigured before them. His face shone like the sun, and his clothes became as white as the light. 3 Just then there appeared before them Moses and Elijah, talking with Jesus. 4 Peter said to Jesus, "Lord, it is good for us to be here. If you wish, I will put up three shelters—one for you, one for Moses and one for Elijah." 5 While he was still speaking, a bright cloud enveloped them, and a voice from the cloud said, "This is my Son, whom I love; with him I am well pleased. Listen to him!" 6 When the disciples heard this, they fell facedown to the ground, terrified. 7 But Jesus came and touched them. "Get up," he said. "Don't be afraid." 8 When they looked up, they saw no one except Jesus.

Mt 22:41 While the Pharisees were gathered together, Jesus asked them, 42 "What do you think about the Christ? Whose son is he?"

"The son of David," they replied. 43 He said to them, "How is it then that David, speaking by the Spirit, calls him 'Lord'? For he says, 44 "'The Lord said to my Lord: "Sit at my right hand until I put your enemies under your feet.'" 45 If then David calls him 'Lord,' how can he be his son?" 46 No one could say a word in reply, and from that day on no one dared to ask him any more questions.

Mt 26:6 While Jesus was in Bethany in the home of a man known as Simon the Leper, 7 a woman came to him with an alabaster jar of very expensive perfume, which she poured on his head as he was reclining at the table. 8 When the disciples saw this, they were indignant. "Why this waste?" they asked. 9 "This perfume could have been sold at a high price and the money given to the poor." 10 Aware of this, Jesus said to them, "Why are you bothering this woman? She has done a beautiful thing to me. 11 The poor you will always have with you, but you will not always have me. 12 When she poured this perfume on my body, she did it to prepare me for burial. 13 I tell you the truth, wherever this gospel is preached throughout the world, what she has done will also be told, in memory of her."

Mt 26:17 On the first day of the Feast of Unleavened Bread, the disciples came to Jesus and asked, "Where do you want us to make preparations for you to eat the Passover?" 18 He replied, "Go into the city to a certain man and tell him, 'The Teacher says: My appointed time is near. I am going to celebrate the Passover with my disciples at your house.'" 19 So the disciples did as Jesus had directed them and prepared the Passover. 20 When evening came, Jesus was reclining at the table with the Twelve. 21 And while they were eating, he said, "I tell you the truth, one of you will betray me." 22 They were very sad and began to say to him one after the other, "Surely not I, Lord?" 23 Jesus replied, "The one who has dipped his hand into the bowl with me will betray me. 24 The Son of Man will go just as it is written about him. But woe to that man who betrays the Son of Man! It would be better for him if he had not been born." 25 Then Judas, the one who would betray him, said, "Surely not I, Rabbi?" Jesus answered, "Yes, it is you." 26 While they were eating, Jesus took bread, gave thanks and broke it, and gave it to his disciples, saying, "Take and eat; this is my body." 27

Scriptures

Then he took the cup, gave thanks and offered it to them, saying, "Drink from it, all of you. 28 This is my blood of the covenant, which is poured out for many for the forgiveness of sins. 29 I tell you, I will not drink of this fruit of the vine from now on until that day when I drink it anew with you in my Father's kingdom."

Mt 26:36 Then Jesus went with his disciples to a place called Gethsemane, and he said to them, "Sit here while I go over there and pray." 37 He took Peter and the two sons of Zebedee along with him, and he began to be sorrowful and troubled. 38 Then he said to them, "My soul is overwhelmed with sorrow to the point of death. Stay here and keep watch with me." 39 Going a little farther, he fell with his face to the ground and prayed, "My Father, if it is possible, may this cup be taken from me. Yet not as I will, but as you will." 40 Then he returned to his disciples and found them sleeping. "Could you men not keep watch with me for one hour?" he asked Peter. 41 "Watch and pray so that you will not fall into temptation. The spirit is willing, but the body is weak." 42 He went away a second time and prayed, "My Father, if it is not possible for this cup to be taken away unless I drink it, may your will be done." 43 When he came back, he again found them sleeping, because their eyes were heavy. 44 So he left them and went away once more and prayed the third time, saying the same thing. 45 Then he returned to the disciples and said to them, "Are you still sleeping and resting? Look, the hour is near, and the Son of Man is betrayed into the hands of sinners. 46 Rise, let us go! Here comes my betrayer!"

Mt. 26:63 But Jesus remained silent. The high priest said to him, "I charge you under oath by the living God: Tell us if you are the Christ, the Son of God." 64 "Yes, it is as you say," Jesus replied. "But I say to all of you: In the future you will see the Son of Man sitting at the right hand of the Mighty One and coming on the clouds of heaven."

Mt. 27:11 Meanwhile Jesus stood before the governor, and the governor asked him, "Are you the king of the Jews?" "Yes, it is as you say," Jesus replied. 12 When he was accused by the chief priests and the elders, he gave no answer. 13 Then Pilate asked him, "Don't you hear the testimony they are bringing against you?"

Mt 27:46 About the ninth hour Jesus cried out in a loud voice, "Eloi, Eloi, lama sabachthani?"—which means, "My God, my God,

Relationship

why have you forsaken me?"

Mt 28:8 So the women hurried away from the tomb, afraid yet filled with joy, and ran to tell his disciples. 9 Suddenly Jesus met them. "Greetings," he said. They came to him, clasped his feet and worshiped him. 10 Then Jesus said to them, "Do not be afraid. Go and tell my brothers to go to Galilee; there they will see me."

Jn 6:35 Then Jesus declared, "I am the bread of life. He who comes to me will never go hungry, and he who believes in me will never be thirsty.

Jn 8:12 When Jesus spoke again to the people, he said, "I am the light of the world. Whoever follows me will never walk in darkness, but will have the light of life."

Jn 8:58 "I tell you the truth," Jesus answered, "before Abraham was born, I am!"

Jn 10:9 I am the gate; whoever enters through me will be saved. He will come in and go out, and find pasture.

Jn 10:14 "I am the good shepherd; I know my sheep and my sheep know me

Jn 11:25 Jesus said to her, "I am the resurrection and the life. He who believes in me will live, even though he dies

Jn 14:6 Jesus answered, "I am the way and the truth and the life. No one comes to the Father except through me.

Jn 15:1 "I am the true vine, and my Father is the gardener.

Pr. 20:5 The purposes of a man's heart are deep waters, but a man of understanding draws them out.

Ro 1:11 I long to see you so that I may impart to you some spiritual gift to make you strong— 12 that is, that you and I may be mutually encouraged by each other's faith.

Jas 5:16 Therefore confess your sins to each other and pray for each other so that you may be healed. The prayer of a righteous man is powerful and effective.

Jos 7:7 And Joshua said, "Ah, Sovereign LORD, why did you ever bring this people across the Jordan to deliver us into the hands of the Amorites to destroy us? If only we had been content to stay on the other side of the Jordan! 8 O Lord, what can I say, now that Israel has been routed by its enemies? 9 The Canaanites and the other people of the country will hear about this and they will surround us and wipe out our name from the earth. What then will

you do for your own great name?"
Ps 25:14 The LORD confides in those who fear him; he makes his covenant known to them. 15 My eyes are ever on the LORD, for only he will release my feet from the snare.

Chapter 16: The Bridge of Trust Scriptures

Ps 65:5 You answer us with awesome deeds of righteousness, O God our Savior, the hope of all the ends of the earth and of the farthest seas
Is 26:4 Trust in the LORD forever, for the LORD, the LORD, is the Rock eternal.
Na 1:7 The LORD is good, a refuge in times of trouble. He cares for those who trust in him
Ps 36:7 How priceless is your unfailing love! Both high and low among men find refuge in the shadow of your wings.
1 Tim 6:17 For we brought nothing into the world, and we can take nothing out of it.
1 Pe 5:7 Cast all your anxiety on him because he cares for you.
Ps 9:10 Those who know your name will trust in you, for you, LORD, have never forsaken those who seek you.
2 Cor 1:10 He has delivered us from such a deadly peril, and he will deliver us. On him we have set our hope that he will continue to deliver us
Ps 5:11 But let all who take refuge in you be glad; let them ever sing for joy. Spread your protection over them, that those who love your name may rejoice in you.
Ps 32:10 Many are the woes of the wicked, but the LORD's unfailing love surrounds the man who trusts in him.
Ps 37:5 Commit your way to the LORD; trust in him and he will do this:
Ps 37:40 The LORD helps them and delivers them; he delivers them from the wicked and saves them, because they take refuge in him.
Ps 125:1 Those who trust in the LORD are like Mount Zion, which cannot be shaken but endures forever.
Pr 16:20 Whoever gives heed to instruction prospers, and blessed is he who trusts in the LORD.

Pr 28:25 A greedy man stirs up dissension, but he who trusts in the LORD will prosper.
Pr 29:25 Fear of man will prove to be a snare, but whoever trusts in the LORD is kept safe.
Is 26:3 You will keep in perfect peace him whose mind is steadfast, because he trusts in you.
Is 57:13 When you cry out for help, let your collection [of idols] save you! The wind will carry all of them off, a mere breath will blow them away. But the man who makes me his refuge will inherit the land and possess my holy mountain."

About BridgeBuilder Ministries International

The primary purpose of **BridgeBuilder Ministries International** is to build relational bridges, connecting people to impact the world for Christ. When Jesus was asked, "What is the greatest commandment?" He replied, "Love the Lord your God with all your heart, with all your soul and with all your mind. This is the first and greatest commandment. And the second is like it, love your neighbor as yourself." BMI will strive to fulfill these commands by equipping people to build interpersonal relationships based on the vital biblical principle of putting God first.

To accomplish our purpose we offer a conference, ***Building Bridges to Connect People***. This conference can be tailored to meet the needs of a range of groups including churches, families and corporate organizations. Components of the conference will focus on relationship building, discipleship, and leadership training designed to inspire attendees to develop vibrant and meaningful relationships with Christ and others.

The hectic pace of today's lifestyle wrecks havoc on relationships. Families pulled in multiple directions for school, work, church, and other activities do not make communicating and re
lating a priority. The result: they are falling apart. As believers co-labor to meet staggering needs both inside and outside the church their relationships can also be tested and strained.

The need is great. We were created as relational beings. We need each other. The ministry of BMI seeks to facilitate a restoration of biblical balance to the many relationships we have.

For information about BMI, to sign up for their mailings, or to share how God has used this book in your life, please write to BMI at:

BridgeBuilder Ministries International
42 Goldenrod Drive
Whispering Pines NC 28327
910 949 3318
www.bmiconnect.org